Psychoanalysis and Other Disciplines Confront Prejudice

Psychoanalysis and Other Disciplines Confront Prejudice: Discrimination Against the Other presents interdisciplinary perspectives on prejudice.

This book considers both the negative and positive implications of *a priori* transmission of values and knowledge. It examines various aspects of prejudice from the perspectives of psychoanalysis, biology, sociology and law. The contributors consider prejudice to be a judgement that precedes experience; it organises and discriminates the events and facts we must assess to understand the world around us, thereby helping us make sense of the world of words, concepts, networks and values into which we are born. Chapters cover a range of topics such as racism, superstition, discrimination and prejudice in psychoanalytic practice. This volume provides a path-breaking treatment of prejudice and how it affects our lives and interactions with others.

Psychoanalysts in training and in practice will find this book a vital resource.

Fanny Blanck-Cereijido is an Argentine psychoanalyst who has practised and taught in Mexico City since 1976. She is a member of the Freudian Society of Mexico City, the Buenos Aires Psychoanalytic Association and the International Psychoanalytic Association. She is a founding member and faculty of the Freudian Society of Mexico City. Dr Blanck-Cereijido is the author of many books and has written extensively about prejudice, the Other and gender.

"The COVID-19 pandemic and the US Black Lives Matter movement have surfaced deep enduring structural discrimination and its dire consequences. *Psychoanalysis and Other Disciplines Confront Prejudice: Discrimination Against the Other* provides a timely exploration of the feelings and thinking that lead to hatred between humans. It thoughtfully exposes how discrimination provides a sense of belonging. Consequently, discrimination becomes even more prevalent and brutal when identity is threatened.

Fanny Blanck-Cereijido has done a masterful job drawing together outstanding authors from diverse fields to contribute to this multidisciplinary and complex study which includes psychoanalytic, cultural, social, philosophical, and medical perspectives. The book offers a broad vision to the reader with which to confront the multiple dimensions of prejudice. Prejudice is transmitted from generation to generation and this book attempts to challenge that transmission by helping readers understand the unconscious processes which drive it. In a time of pandemic, war, forced migrations and exile, it is a magnificent contribution toward a world of peace and tolerance."

Adriana Prengler, *Vice-President of the International Psychoanalytical Association*

"Prejudice is inherent to the subject and to groups. It's based on a rejection of the new, the foreign, the alien, and the not known. Prejudice relates to systems of belief, of faith, and it is the support for racist and discriminatory thoughts. This book problematizes the topic of prejudice and analyzes in depth the different meanings it has for clinical and theoretical psychoanalysis, biology, and conductism. It is conceived as a complex system."

Janine Puget, *Psychoanalyst of the de la Asociación Psicoanalítica de Buenos Aires (2014)*

Psychoanalysis and Other Disciplines Confront Prejudice

Discrimination Against the Other

Edited by
Fanny Blanck-Cereijido

R Routledge
Taylor & Francis Group

LONDON AND NEW YORK

Designed cover image: Getty Images | wildpixel

First published in English 2023
by Routledge
4 Park Square, Milton Park, Abingdon, Oxon OX14 4RN

and by Routledge
605 Third Avenue, New York, NY 10158

Routledge is an imprint of the Taylor & Francis Group, an informa business

El Siglo del Prejuicio Confrontado by Fanny Blanck-Cereijido
© 2014 Paradiso editores S.A. de C.V. (México)

© Gerardo Piña for the translation of the following chapters: "Foreword" by Fanny
Blanck-Cereijido; "Thought and Reality in Prejudice, Superstition and Collective
Delusion" by Juan Vives Rocabert; "Prejudice and Racism" by Olivia Gall; "Prejudice
as a Basis for Discrimination" by Fanny Blanck-Cereijido; "Prejudice and Its Effects on
the Psychoanalytic Clinic" by Miriam Grynberg Robinson; "The Logic of Prejudice" by
Ulises Schmill Ordóñez; and "Biological Roots of Prejudice" by Marcelino Cereijido.

Published in Spanish by Paradiso editores 2014

Trademark notice: Product or corporate names may be trademarks or registered
trademarks, and are used only for identification and explanation without intent to infringe.

British Library Cataloguing in Publication Data
A catalogue record for this book is available from the British Library

Library of Congress Cataloging-in-Publication Data
Names: Blanck de Cereijido, Fanny, editor.
Title: Psychoanalysis and other disciplines confront prejudice :
discrimination against the other / edited by Fanny Blanck Cereijido.
Other titles: Siglo del prejuicio confrontado. English
Description: Abingdon, Oxon ; New York, NY : Routledge, 2023. |
Originally published in Spanish as El Siglo del prejucio confrontado by Pardiso
Editores in 2014. | Includes bibliographical references and index. |
Identifiers: LCCN 2022027688 (print) | LCCN 2022027689 (ebook) |
ISBN 9781032272535 (paperback) | ISBN 9781032272542 (hardback) |
ISBN 9781003291978 (ebook)
Subjects: LCSH: Prejudices--Social aspects. | Racism. | Discrimination.
Classification: LCC HM1091 .S5413 2023 (print) | LCC HM1091 (ebook) |
DDC 303.3/85--dc23/eng/20220716
LC record available at https://lccn.loc.gov/2022027688
LC ebook record available at https://lccn.loc.gov/2022027689

ISBN: 978-1-032-27254-2 (hbk)
ISBN: 978-1-032-27253-5 (pbk)
ISBN: 978-1-003-29197-8 (ebk)

DOI: 10.4324/9781003291978

Typeset in Times New Roman
by Taylor & Francis Books

Contents

Contributors

Juan Vives Rocabert is a surgeon (UNAM), psychiatrist (Division of Higher Studies of UNAM, Mexican Council of Psychiatry, Mexican Society of Neurology and Psychiatry, Mexican Psychiatric Association), psychoanalyst and lecturer (Mexican Psychoanalytic Association), and group psychotherapist (Mexican Association of Group Analytic Psychotherapy). He has written 15 books and 60 book chapters. He is the author of more than 150 psychoanalytical works, as well as 100 journalistic articles. He was president and director of the Institute of the Mexican Psychoanalytic Association, secretary of the Latin American Federation of Psychoanalysis, member of the Council Board of the International Psychoanalytic Association, associate editor of the *International Journal of Psycho-Analysis*, of the annual book of psychoanalysis and associate director of the Latin American Institute of Psychoanalysis.

Email: juanvives@prodigy.net.mx

Olivia Gall received her BA in Sociology from the Faculty of Political and Social Sciences, UNAM (1980), and her MA (1981) and PhD (1986) in Political Science from the Institut d'Etudes Politiques, France. She is a senior researcher at the CEIICH-UNAM and has given numerous lectures and papers at national and international conferences, as well as publishing several articles, book chapters and books (as editor) on racism in Mexico and Latin America, from a theoretical and historical perspective.

Email: olivgall@unam.mx

Fanny Blanck-Cereijido qualified as a Doctor of Medicine at the Faculty of Medicine of the University of Buenos Aires. She received psychoanalytic training in Buenos Aires, Boston and Mexico and is a full member of the Buenos Aires Psychoanalytic Association and a full teaching member of the Mexican Psychoanalytic Association. She has published books and articles on female sexuality, assisted reproduction, Freud's relationship with Judaism, authoritarianism, the transmission of psychoanalysis, time, death, otherness and foreignness, survival conditions in extreme situations, and the problematic of evil and prejudice.

Email: cereijidofanny@gmail.com

Silvia Amati Sas, Doctor of Medicine (University of Buenos Aires), specialised in child psychiatry in Geneva with Professor Julián de Ajuriaguerra and did her psychoanalytic training at the Swiss Psychoanalytic Society, of which she is a teaching member. She is a full member of the Italian Psychoanalytic Association. She has written articles on traumatic social violence, conformism, shame, countertransference, and ethics in the therapeutic work of extreme situations and prejudice.

Email: amatisas@teletu.it

Miriam Grynberg Robinson is a psychoanalyst and teacher belonging to the Mexican Psychoanalytic Association (APM) and the International Psychoanalytic Association. She has BA and MA degrees in Psychology from the Universidad Iberoamaricana. She is a professor in the postgraduate and psychoanalytic training courses of the APM and has published articles on the psychoanalysis of prejudice, transgenerational transmission and trauma.

Email: miriamgc32@hotmail.com

Ulises Schmill has been a magistrate at the Federal Tax Court, Mexican ambassador to Austria, Hungary and the Federal Republic of Germany, and president of the Supreme Court of Justice of the Nation (1991–1994). He has been a university professor for more than 40 years and currently teaches general theory of law at the Instituto Tecnológico Autónomo de México. His works include *El debate sobre Mitilene* (DOXA, 1987), *Lógica y derecho* (Fontamara, 1993), *Teoría del derecho y del Estado* (Porrúa, 2003), *La conducta del jabalí, Dos ensayos sobre el poder, Kafka y Shakespeare* and *Las revoluciones: teoría jurídica y consideraciones sociológicas* (Trotta, 2009).

Email: uschmill@itam.mx

Marcelino Cereijido is physician and Doctor of Medicine (University of Buenos Aires), Professor Emeritus of Cellular and Molecular Physiology at the Centro de Investigación y de Estudios Avanzados and National Researcher Emeritus. Apart from his publications relating to his profession, he has published, among other books: *La vida, el tiempo y la muerte* (FCE, 2002, 3rd ed.), *La muerte y sus ventajas* (FCE, 2002, 3rd ed.), both with Fanny Blanck-Cereijido, and *Hacia una teoría general de los hijos de puta* (Tusquets, 2011), among others.

Email: marcelinocereijido@gmail.com

Foreword

The first version of *El siglo del prejuicio confrontado* was published in 2014. That shows our collective awareness and anticipatory intuition regarding the urgent need for discussion of prejudice. The following years have witnessed a huge increase in consciousness and a historic confrontation of prejudice – mainly regarding race and gender.

The inequality with which people experienced the COVID-19 pandemic, combined with horrific acts of discrimination such as George Floyd's murder, triggered social outrage. That rendered confrontation of and grappling with prejudice unavoidable. This is evident in the confrontations now taking place in all academic fields and institutions, business life, professional life, cultural life and politics.

Unfortunately, because the book was written in Spanish, it was unknown to English-speaking readers. I hope this translation helps spread these important and original insights from Latin American thinkers on this critical subject.

Acknowledgements

I am very grateful to my daughter, Margarita Cereijido, and to my son-in-law, Thomas Palley, for encouraging and helping me with this translation project. They have been the engine driving this work.

Introduction

The Century of Confronted Prejudice

Fanny Blanck-Cereijido

Prejudice is understood as discriminatory and derogatory ideas towards a subject, a community, a country or a social group. The issue of discrimination encompasses the individual psyche and the social imaginary, as each society is constituted of its values, its concept of justice, logic and aesthetics, so that it seems that the inferiority of the Other is the reverse of the affirmation of one's own truth; from here there is a short distance to others being attributed an evil and perverse essence.[1]

The term *prejudice* implies the idea of a judgement that precedes one's own experience, which corresponds to the Kantian a priori, gathers the beliefs, values and reference categories of the world of each subject and depends on the words and concepts in which that subject is born and will be immersed. It also provides an order and discrimination of the facts and factors that each person must evaluate in order to understand the world around them and is therefore essential for thought and helps to protect self-definition and one's own limits. This classification prior to individual judgement places beliefs and convictions in a system of values accepted or rejected by the family and society that precede that individual. In this way they are conditioned in their beliefs and values by their family and social belonging, which in turn are the effect of conscious and unconscious transgenerational transmission.

The certainties provided by prejudices are uncritically incorporated beliefs, immovable traditions.[2] On the other hand, the judgement described by Freud as "judgement of attribution and existence" allows us to discriminate, attribute values, establish categories and distinguish an external object from an internal one, as well as being modifiable by new knowledge or reasoning.

Human beings have always been prejudiced, as there are evolutionary and cultural factors that condition them to be this way, and there is no record of any society that has not been so.

When the one who assigns a negative value to a community or group with characteristics that are foreign to them possesses the force to exercise discrimination, contempt and violence, we are faced with malignant prejudice. The wielder of prejudice and destructive force will attack and eliminate the object of hatred and contempt.

DOI: 10.4324/9781003291978-1

It is important to find the specific events or situations that link common prejudices, such as preferences, affinities and customs, with malignant forms of violence and destruction.

From a biological perspective, when some structural or behavioural attribute is observed in all the peoples of the Earth and through all generations since the dawn of history, some important advantage is granted to those who express it, otherwise natural selection would not have chosen it and globalised it. In this way, prejudice has basically two aspects—it is known through the negative consequences that it undoubtedly causes, and these are so many, so serious and painful, that they have preponderated. But we must also comprehend the functions that prejudice has in order to understand why it has been selected so effectively.[3]

The human tool par excellence, to fight for life, arises from an enormous hypertrophy of the capacity to know, the development of which has been accompanied by the *co-selection of the believer*.[4] Being a believer allows each new individual to inherit through upbringing, education and life in society all that has been learned by previous generations. Having been selected for being believers, we will be depositaries and continuers of universal knowledge and thought, but also of a burden of prejudices that may have some advantage, as I said at the beginning, but for the time being they highlight the despicable. Charles Darwin stated: "A belief constantly inculcated during the early years of life, when the brain is very impressionable, acquires almost the nature of an instinct: it is obeyed independently of reason."

A little over a decade ago, on the occasion of the transition from the 20th to the 21st century, there were many attempts to characterise the 20th century by giving it subtitles. "It was the century of the atom", because, although the pre-Socratic Democritus of Abdera had asserted that the atom was indivisible, the physicists of the 20th century were breaking it down into a subparticle of such inconceivable smallness that they gave free rein to their frustration at not finding it. The Nobel Prize in Physics laureate, Leon Max Lederman, wanted to call it *"the goddam particle"*,[5] but—cowardly and pusillanimous—the editor of a journal would not allow him to do so, and they ended up calling it "the God particle", a nickname more in keeping with their prejudices. "It was the century of the genome", as the genetic message that holds the secret of life was decoded. "It was the century of the universe", for we realised that, instead of living in a single galaxy, the Milky Way, we live in a universe in which it is just one among millions and millions of similar nebulae. "It was the century of surgery", for, by the end of the 19th century, the great physicians had predicted that the brain, the heart and the abdomen could never be operated on. "It was the century of communication", for today we watch a football match played on the other side of the planet from our armchair at home. "It was the century of the unconscious", because, although Sigmund Freud's discoveries and developments had begun in the 19th century, psychoanalysis invaded the psychic, medical, artistic and educational spheres, the interpretation of society and history, among many others. "It was the century of the woman", because, whereas in the 19th century women still did not vote and were not allowed to enter universities, in the 20th century women scientists, writers, composers, athletes and leaders flourished. "It was the century of the child", because they went from being "miniature madmen", as Joan Manuel Serrat called them, to having a mind that developed in stages that Jean Piaget began to find, characterise and decipher, because at no stage are they mad or stupid; on the contrary, once the most harmful prejudices had been eliminated, it was found that children have an overwhelming logic at all times.

Suddenly, owing to a combination of factors, the details of which we will not go into here, the 20th century traveller was not the daring adventurer on board his caravel, but the ordinary citizen, the business commission agent, the tourist, the scholarship holder, the Mexican boxer who was going to fight for a title against a Filipino, or the chess player who was going to play against an Indian grandmaster; communication, cinema, literature, migration, intercontinental wars, Olympic Games, world championships brought extremely diverse human beings face to face and forced them to sell, buy, visit, live together, meet in international congresses and societies, compete in football or swimming, exhibit their paintings and sculptures and show them theirs, as well as debate in the same forums. It would not be an exaggeration to say that, in the course of the 20th century, human beings went from imagining and thinking about each other to seeing, hearing and interacting directly with each other. Kant may have got away with it, for we will never know the noumenal reality of the "other", but the 20th century has brought us close enough to meet them face to face! It is then that we discover that, in order to understand others, we have to try to free them from the tangle of confusion, ignorance and prejudice with which we have been distorting them for millennia.

The huge human task now is to see how far this new "reality" matches what we had pre-imagined and to decide what to do with the discrepancies. We must hasten to dismantle the prejudices, at least by the time we are the ones who arrive in their land, and they are the ones who try to force us to accept the idea they had made of us. The 20th century threw us into a new situation, a scenario full of "others", and now, in the 21st century, we have to learn to rescue them from that cloud of prejudice in which we lived immersed, to change with all haste the-glass-through-which-we-look-at-them. In this sense, we believe that we could subtitle the 20th century as "the century of confronted prejudice". Unfortunately, this does not mean that confronting our old ideas with new realities will cure us of being prejudiced. After all, an athlete was once stripped of his Olympic medals because he was found to be indigenous, women were excluded from higher education, a poet was imprisoned for being gay, women are still stoned because a man raped them, but a jury (made up of macho men, needless to say) assumed that the virtuous male was forced by the irresistible and unforgivable seductress, and yet, in the 21st century, as soon as a people deem it convenient, they continue to massacre entire villages for fabricated reasons. These shameful horrors emanate from prejudices that have unconscious components, and the solution to them is not exclusively within the reach of education and culture.

As the 20th century has already passed, we can affirm that the title of this book is not a kind of hopeful prediction: the confrontation between the prejudiced, who have not only the prejudices but also the power to impose them, and the Other, the victim, has already begun and, as we enter the 21st century, it continues in full force. But it is obvious that multidisciplinary analysis and social struggle are trying to achieve a rethinking of the criteria and strategy with which prejudice is approached. First, it is no longer restricted to the realm of conscience, or that of ethics, and it has been shown that pre-prejudice may not allude to a shoddy use of reasoning, but, on the contrary, to a fine logic cunningly designed to confuse the judgement of the prejudiced (enthymeme). Second, prejudice configures what is nowadays called a "complex system". This is a new theoretical scaffolding for approaching systems that include objects and processes of a diverse nature—for example, health care depends on medical knowledge, but also on available money, social organisation, trade unions, administrative rules, political system, religious beliefs, and so on.[6]

The same applies when we look at education, trade, sport, war. It should be noted that complication is not enough. For example, the famous clock in Strasbourg cathedral has around 5,000 parts that mark the time, the day, the phases of the moon, the seasons and countless other variables. Yet it is not considered *complex*, but merely *complicated*, because its functioning can be explained by only one discipline: mechanics. "Complex" systems, on the other hand, require that their various facets be dealt with by various disciplines, and it is obvious that the confrontation forcedly unravelled in the 20th century has biological, educational, economic, political, class, legal, gender, as well as other aspects. In Chapter 8, we will see that complex systems also exhibit *emergent properties*—that is, properties that could not have been foreseen from the study of their separate components, but we bring them up because it is possible that at least part of the reason for the violent and irremissible rejection of the Other lies in the effort to prevent it from contaminating the human groups that come together for a purpose and generate emergent properties.

That is why I thought it appropriate to invite leading specialists from different disciplines, such as sociology, philosophy, law and biology, who have been studying prejudice from different perspectives. While this approach is essential, given the complex systemic nature of the phenomenon of prejudice, it avoids the typical parochialism that sooner or later obscures disciplines that become entrenched in their criteria.

The fact that the roots of prejudice have a strong unconscious component does not bode well for its eradication in the foreseeable future. But, even so, the study of prejudice simplifies the understanding of current paradigms. The confrontation carried out during the 20th century has succeeded in bringing about inadmissible human situations owing to prejudice. As, at the end of the same century, many of these situations had been confronted, it shows that the effort made in multidisciplinary analysis and social struggle has had significant achievements for the first time in many millennia.

Notes

1 Cornelius Castoriadis, "Reflections on racism", in *Memoirs of the colloquium "Unconscious and social change"*. Paris, Association pour la recherche et l'intervention psychologique, 1985.
2 Janine Puget, *Correspondance*. IPA Committee on Prejudice (including Anti-Semitism), Working Group, 2009.
3 However, the illustrious evolutionist Ernst Haeckel has lamented: "Passion and selfishness, that is the secret of life".
4 Marcelino Cereijido, *La ciencia como calamidad* (Science as a calamity). Barcelona, Gedisa, 2009.
5 Also known as the Higgs boson.
6 Despite the fact that the greatest medical breakthrough of all time stems from the evolutionary approach, medical schools in developing countries do not teach the subject of evolution because it would conflict with cultures based on religious creationism. In some countries, autopsies are banned, in others, blood transfusions, and so on.

Chapter 1

Thought and Reality in Prejudice, Superstition and Collective Delusion

Juan Vives Rocabert

Introduction

Prejudice is an aprioristic – in Kantian terms – way of approaching the world. As we cannot scrutinise and scientifically investigate each and every one of the beliefs that affect how we conduct ourselves in life, the vast majority of our concepts derive from a belief (doxa) and not from knowledge (episteme). In other words, in everyday life, we orient ourselves on the basis of a series of judgements for which we have no corroboration – that is, non-rational judgements, or prejudgements. As Freud had already stated in a famous example, when discussing the truth of Alexander the Great's existence, it would be highly impractical if every person had to corroborate, again and again, in every generation, each and every piece of knowledge he or she possesses.[1] The principle of authority – including the almost undisputed authority we confer on the written word – is, after all, the opinion of others and it prevails, much more than we would like to admit, in almost every practical aspect of everyday life.

Strictly speaking, prejudices, like superstitions and delusions, have no other origin than such beliefs and involve a psychic mechanism of great economy in practical terms. As we shall see below, superstitions are but a special case of prejudices, and religions are organised and systematised forms of superstition – that is, they are cultural delusional systems, just as Freud proposed at the time. Hence, almost all authors agree that prejudice is part of human nature, of so-called normal psychic processes. Strictly speaking, it is part of that tendency to settle questions of thought in closer contact with the pleasure principle – more in line with our desires – than with the reality principle.

Prejudices and superstitions – such as religious thinking – are transmitted primarily through the family, the social group and the culture to which the subject belongs. This is possible because, in principle, we believe that what the family teaches us is not only true but also good. This belief constitutes a particularly economical – in metapsychological terms – means of conducting oneself through life. The acceptance and incorporation of the beliefs of the social and cultural group into which one is born provide a kind of guarantee of truth of great psychic economy in relation to our vision of the world and

DOI: 10.4324/9781003291978-2

the people around us, those close and known, as well as those far away and strangers. The functioning of the groups into which we are born dictates that what comes from the in-group is good, safe, healthy and true; in contrast, what comes from the out-group is bad, dangerous, unsafe and must be fought against in order to preserve security. Hence the proverbial distrust of the outsider. It is enough that an outsider does not behave, in the face of his mother's death, as the norms sanctioned by custom dictate for his behaviour to be censured and for him to be considered inadequate and dangerous – as Albert Camus well knew.[2]

We understand that the transmission of prejudices and superstitions, together with other criteria and ways of thinking, such as cultural, ethical, aesthetic, religious and political values, can occur by conscious means, but also unconscious. The generational transmission of such conceptual contents can occur without either the transmitters or the receivers of such prejudices being aware of the unconscious communication process. It is very likely that the psychic mechanisms of introjective identification and projective identification described by M. Klein are responsible for this form of unconscious generational transmission.[3] This mode of transmission implies, for the generation that receives what is transmitted, an enormous saving of energy, as it does not have to learn experimentally and on its own what previous generations transmit to it; however, this *knowledge* includes all sorts of prejudices; erroneous, false or distorted concepts; superstitions; religious myths; political ideologies; ethical precepts; fables; all kinds of animism and magical thinking; and so on. A very important part of the *Weltanshauung* – the world-view – by which we orient ourselves in existence includes a long list of these acquisitions. There are authors who, from the point of view of the transmission of ideologies, think that this kind of transmission serves the interests of the state; thus – as Louis Althuser says – religion, school, but mainly the family, are ideological apparatuses of the state in the service of the ruling class and serve to perpetuate it.[4]

Despite the universality of the above stated, the vast majority of researchers of this phenomenon, based mainly on racial or social prejudice, have pointed out that ignorance is indebted to prejudice, and that knowledge dissolves prejudice; however, the fact remains that prejudice very often replaces knowledge. In Aristotle's terms, doxa replaces episteme: opinion – belief – takes the place of knowledge. Prejudice, based on opinion, is almost the rule in everyday life and constitutes a way to save oneself the arduous path of acquiring knowledge, which is rather scarce and difficult to acquire.

On the other hand, it is clear that we consider our beliefs to be correct, truthful or at least adequate; otherwise, we would not believe in them with the certainty that we do. From this follows the eventuality that, very generally speaking, each person thinks and is convinced that his or her criteria, standards, ethics and, in general, whole thought processes are correct. Beyond any consideration of narcissism, it is often the case that, in everyday life, no one holds or considers their criteria, often based on prejudices, to be erroneous, wrong or unethical. This implies the complication that, if the other's thinking is different or divergent from our own, it can automatically fall under the suspicion that it is wrong, false or erroneous. How to reconcile this state of affairs? The obvious answer is that, if the subject uses his or her critical thinking – judgement – he or she will be in a position to access the pros and cons of both his or her own thinking, criteria, ethics and so on and the thinking of the other. However, this does not happen as often as would be desirable, given that prejudices often nest in the unconscious; the opposite is true, in fact, and it is common to deal with aprioristic judgements without paying attention to the possibility of examining or scrutinising the arguments on which these prejudices or beliefs are based. If we bear in mind that science does not have absolute truths, and that, on the contrary, its postulates are always transitory and await further research or information, then we will realise that, in daily life, the mental mechanisms that sustain prejudices are not only everyday but absolutely indispensable.

Another difficulty has to do with the impression we harbour that different, contrasting or unusual thoughts, criteria or concepts must fall under the suspicion of being dangerous or potentially harmful until proven otherwise. Therefore, the uncommon puts us on alert, the strange awakens a certain state of expectant alarm. Thanks to this form of *physiological paranoia*, if I may call it that, and vigilance against any potential predator, many species have survived in the course of evolution. The other may be regarded, in particular, with suspicion until there are clear signs that he or she does not intend us harm or is not a threat. Even in the case of minimal inequalities, we have known since Freud coined the notion of narcissism of small differences that it is not necessary for the other to be different in reality. The unknown neighbour, even if she or he is very similar to ourselves, can fall into the field of our prejudices, simply because she or he belongs to the "exo-familial" group. It is not necessary for skin colour to be different; the other may even belong to the same nation or community, as we know this happens with struggles between different regionalisms in a country. It is common that the other, in all respects similar to ourselves, is nevertheless the repository of that part of ourselves that we do not want to realise and for which we do not want to take responsibility, hence the frequency of the mechanism of projection in the emergence of prejudice.

This also has to do with the fact that we are strangers to ourselves, as a part of our psyche – the unconscious – is alien to our consciousness and, therefore, strange. We have no knowledge of the unconscious desires and fantasies that inhabit us, hence the need to deposit them, projectively, in the other. This resolves the discomfort caused by certain mental contents that we do not wish to take responsibility for because they are embarrassing, are contradictory to other parts of ourselves or conflict with the ethical standards we have incorporated. The mechanism of projection makes us see these representations in the other without simultaneously noticing them in ourselves. This is why it is so useful for the other to be very similar to ourselves:

it facilitates the mechanism by which we get rid of the undesirable, thus being able to see it on the outside.

Let us remember that Freud established that, in the course of development, the infant tends to incorporate all that it considers good and useful, while it spits out that which is not good, which does not nourish it. These biological proto-types are the basis for sustaining the subsequent erotic mechanisms of introjec-tion and projection. In turn, introjection will be the platform for the central mechanism of identification, a fundamental mechanism for the constitution of the subject. Thus, incorporation, introjection and identification form a *continuum* from the biological to the emotional – from the bodily to the psychic. Following this line of thought, Freud established that any stimulus from outside that penetrates the psyche is uncomfortable for the system and must be dislodged as soon as possible: this is the Freudian reflexological basis of the principle of displeasure/pleasure. The problem arises when the stimulus comes from the depths of the somatic and enters the psyche: these are the instinctual drives. In this case, either the defence mechanisms come into action – mainly the repres-sion of instinctual pressure – or an adaptation is made according to the rules of the reality principle, in order to satisfy the instinctual demand.

Based on these elementary mechanisms of incorporation or rejection, we tend to regard everything good as within us, while we label everything external as bad or potentially harmful. From Freud's reasoning and further developments on narcissism, there is only one step to understanding the intimate conviction that we, all of us, are good; while others, all our fellows, are bad. The great economy of the schizo-paranoid mode of thought creates this sense of certainty. It will be necessary to progress a long way in the course of the development of our rea-soning capacity to reach the possibility of understanding and tolerating that the other, being different, is not bad by definition and has a good side, and, conse-quently, that we too, alongside our virtues and goodness, can harbour bad, aggressive and destructive parts, distort reality or be mistaken.

Tolerating our differences from the other is a fundamental part of social coexistence – which does not cancel out the dynamics between the endo-group and the exo-group. The other, with his or her way of being, opinions, criteria, own beliefs and convictions and so on, can question head-on substantive parts of our own identity, can make us see our narrow-mindedness by showing us panoramas never seen before, criteria never contemplated before, ways of thinking – even ways of feeling – that are unheard of in our experience. Strictly speaking, this mechanism also explains to us a central element for the con-stitution of the *self*, such as self-esteem, as well as the structuring of the Ideal of Self, the repository of secondary narcissism.

As Blanck-Cereijido has rightly pointed out, prejudices tend to order the facts and form part of a system of values that pre-exist the individual him- or herself and are transmitted generationally in a conscious and unconscious manner; accepted by the family and the community in which an individual grows up, prejudices uncritically condition his or her beliefs and world-view.

They form part of the tradition of the culture in which the subject grows up.[5] In other words, what we incorporate generationally from our elders – prejudices included – organises our thinking in a certain way, hence the fixity and stability with which prejudices and superstitions remain in the depths of our psyche: they are embedded in our identity cores, they form part of that inherited conceptual universe that guides us in our understanding of the world and its relationships.

The assumption that prejudices and the potential of thought to adhere to prejudices are universal, with a broad empirical basis, guides us in trying to explore what happens in the thinking and judgemental capacity of human beings; how racial, social and class prejudices come about; what the superstitions and taboos are made of by which culture dictates its norms; what is the inner matter of those shared delusions – called religion – with which human beings try to feel safe, cared for and protected under systems where the denial of death suspends, albeit temporarily, the anguish before nothingness, the safest but also the most terrifying event.

But it must be conceded, on the other hand, that prejudice involves a serious distortion of the perceptual function: once a person believes that people of colour or Jews or the French or Americans are evil, wicked or dangerous, this belief tends to be refractory to the evidence of perception; in fact, objective reality is either denied or distorted. Once a person is convinced that a lunar eclipse can cause the foetus of a pregnant woman to be born with a cleft lip and cleft palate, there would seem to be no argument or demonstration to rectify such a belief, and so an amulet to prevent the evil spell is preferred. Prejudice and superstitions are, therefore, a kind of delusional interpretation of what is perceived. Prejudice shares with superstitions and delusions a serious compromise of the judgement of reality and is often irreducible to the ascertainment of perceptions, which, in turn, imposes a serious handicap on the capacity of thought and forms of reasoning of the secondary process, involving a process of delay and an inhibition of the ego's tendency to discharge. As we have already mentioned, from motivations that have to do with unconscious desires, prejudices work against the functioning of the reality principle and support the dynamics of the pleasure principle. In this sense, prejudices, superstitions and religious delusions share a very similar dynamic.

Psychoanalysis and Judgement

As we are talking about prejudice and the judgement of reality, it is necessary to review, however briefly, what psychoanalysis defines as judgemental thinking. One of the most important questions in relation to the function of judgement has to do with the way we process our perceptions and the data contained in our memory. As early as 1895, in "Project of a psychology for neurologists", Freud drew the distinction between *reproductive thinking* and *judicative thinking*. The latter "is a process ψ which only becomes possible through the inhibition exercised by the ego and which is brought about by the dissimilarity between the *desiderative cathexis* of a memory and a *perceptual cathexis* which is similar to it" – in other words, judgement becomes possible only through the inhibition exercised by the ego and is brought about by the dissimilarity between the *desiderative cathexis* of a memory and a *perceptual cathexis* that is similar to it.[6] In other words, judgement is established by being able to distinguish between our desires and the data offered by our perceptual function.

Freud established the two different types of situations that can occur in the ego. The first occurs when the ego, in a state of desire, "re-cathects" the trace of the object and promotes the process of discharge; obviously, satisfaction is not achieved with this discharge as the object does not exist in reality, it has only been hallucinated. At first, ψ cannot make the distinction and needs help to distinguish between a perception and a representation. In the second situation, ψ needs a sign that directs his or her attention to the "re-cathectisation" of the hostile mnemic trace and thus enables him or her to prevent the triggering of displeasure thanks to the collateral cathexes. Therefore, in order to distinguish perception from representation (a central element for the judgement of reality), the help of perceptual φ-neurons is needed to supply the sign of reality. With each external perception, a qualitative excitation is produced in the ω-neurons. And it is precisely this perceptual discharge coming to ψ from the ω-neurons that constitutes the sign of quality or reality for ψ.

When the mnemic trace of the desired object is catechised, a hallucination is produced and it gives a sign of discharge or reality as if it were an external perception. Here, the differentiation between perception and mnemic trace or representation fails. But, if the cathexis on the desired object is inhibited, then it will not produce a sign of quality, unlike the perception of the external object. This difference lies in the fact that, in the perception of the external object, the quality sign always appears, regardless of the intensity of the cathexis, whereas the one coming from ψ will only occur when the investiture is very intense.

It is, therefore, inhibition from the ego that provides the criterion for making a distinction between perception and recollection. When the I is in a state of desire at the moment when the sign of reality arises, it will promote the discharge to be directed in the direction of the specific action. In contrast, if the sign of reality coincides with an increase of displeasure, ψ will produce a defence in order to avoid pain, thanks to a collateral cathexis. The cathexis of desire carried through to hallucination and the total triggering of displeasure, which promotes the full deployment of the defence, are the phenomena Freud referred to as *primary psychic processes*. The processes made possible by a good cathexis of ψ – that is, those that are attenuated variations of the primary psychic processes – are the *secondary psychic processes* – those that involve a correct use of the signs of reality, of inhibition on the part of the ego (aspects that he would explain more clearly later in *The Interpretation of Dreams*).

As we can see, this would be, from the Freudian terminology used in the "Project of a psychology for neurologists", the existing distinction between *desiderative thinking* (linked to the pleasure principle and the primary process) and *judicative thinking* (linked to the reality principle and the secondary process). This is why we have stated above that prejudice – as well as superstition and delusion – is a form of thought close to the primary process, as all these have much more to do with desiderative thought than with judicative thought.

When the cathexis of desire in the mnemic trace is accompanied by the perception of the object of the memory in reality, then the cathexes are superimposed, and a sign of reality arises in the ω-neurons that leads to an effective discharge theorisation which will be complemented by the considerations set out in "The Negation", of 1925. When the cathexis of the mnemic trace of desire does not completely coincide with that of the perception of the object, then a function is established, which is judgement. Judgement establishes, on the one hand, the resemblance that really exists between the core of the ego and the perceived, and, on the other hand, between the distinct elements. In this sense, Freud distinguishes between "the thing" and its activity or attributes: its predicate.

Thus, judgement is the process that makes it possible to distinguish, thanks to the inhibition exercised by the ego, between the desiderative cathexis of a memory and the perceptive cathexis of something similar. The coincidence between the cathexes provides a biological signal that puts an end to thought (the cognitive act) and initiates discharge. Conversely, when the cathexes do not coincide, the thought process arises. Freud exemplifies this when an infant looks at the breast from the front and from the side, so that thought and action (moving the head) combine to achieve the required identity for two images that might seemingly refer to different objects. The aim of the above is to achieve a sense of identity. This is achieved by shifting the quantity $Q\eta$ in every possible way. "The struggle between fixed facilitations and fluctuating cathexes characterises the secondary process of reproductive thinking."[7]

Also fundamental to the development and establishment of the judgement of reality is the concept of the resemblance complex, which leads to the possibility of establishing the closeness between "the thing" (the outside) and the memory of "the thing" in the body (the inside). This process, consisting of analysing a perceptual complex, leads to a (re)knowledge of the object and implies a judgement; it comes to an end once this latter end has been achieved. As we can see, it is the primitive interest in establishing the situation of satisfaction that leads, in one case, to *reproductive reflection* and, in the other, to *judgement*.

In concluding his essay, Freud established that both reproductive thinking and judicative thinking pursue an identity with a bodily cathexis. Reproductive thought pursues identity with a psychic cathexis (an experience of the subject), while judicative thought operates before reproductive thought. If, at the conclusion of the cognitive act, the sign of reality is added to the perception, a *judgement of reality*, a belief, is achieved. This primary judgement implies a lesser degree of influence from the catechised self than the reproductive acts of thought.

Later in his complementary theorisations, in *The Denial* of 1925, Freud pointed out the distinction, within judicative thought, between the judgement of attribution and the judgement of existence. The former determines what is attributed to the subject: good if it has to do with the inside, bad if it belongs to the external world. This is the origin of considering the other, the stranger or the unknown, as potentially dangerous until proven otherwise. René Spitz's developmental studies confirm this postulate when he describes the infant's 8th-month anguish in the face of a figure that is strange to it, different from the familiarity of the parental figures. When the infant reacts to a stranger, with whom it has never had an unpleasant experience, it does so simply because the figure is different from the mother and, therefore, potentially dangerous.[8]

The judgement of existence, on the other hand, is that which grants the status of existent to someone other than myself and which also distinguishes between a perception that comes from outside and the perception of memory, from the mnemic trace left by the object. The judgement of existence makes it possible for us to distinguish between perception and memory.[9] As scholars of racial prejudice, especially those who have studied anti-Semitism, have noted, racist arguments are based on a mechanism by which a *judgement of non-existence* is achieved in the other, who is transformed into a thing or a number. This mechanism operates by dehumanising the other, declaring him or her non-existent from the perspective of being. This mechanism was pro-totypical, in the last century, of Nazi propaganda in relation to the Jews, dehumanising them and turning them into material to be used and discarded.

As we can see, in the "Project of a psychology for neurologists", Freud established the distinction between the primary process and the secondary process; in the former, there is the hallucination of the object and the discharge, while, in the latter, the delay is established by the inhibition of the ego. All proportion kept, it is as if in prejudice there had been no opportunity to dis-tinguish between the hallucination of the inner world – our desire and, we might add, inherited dictates – and objective reality. The characteristics of the other will be what our inner world and our beliefs determine, something much closer to what we were consciously and unconsciously taught by our parents, teachers or other models during adolescence, and not what we can see, if we want to, in objective reality. Therefore, we can understand prejudice as a mental mechanism very close to the primary process, which does not benefit from the considerations usually taken into account by the secondary process.

By virtue of what we have explored above, we understand that beliefs (doxa) are strongly sifted by our desires and determined by the pleasure principle, while knowledge (episteme) derives from the approaches we make to objectivity guided by the reality principle. If a human being is defined by his or her desires, then we can venture the conjecture that prejudices define human beings. A human being *is* his or her prejudices – that is, his or her desires.

Prejudice

Prejudice is usually defined as a way of "judging things before the appropriate time, or without having full knowledge of them".[10] José Ferrater Mora defines it "as a judgement prior to, or before, adequate or full knowledge of a thing".[11] It is interesting, this author tells us, how numerous philosophical currents have concluded that prejudices are practically unavoidable, even impossible to avoid, going so far as to affirm that the only way to avoid them is to abstain from making any kind of judgement. José Ortega y Gasset, who prefers to speak of beliefs as synonymous with prejudices, establishes that these are formulated before or independently of judgement; therefore, knowledge – eventually – can undo beliefs or prejudices, at least from the perspective of a philosophy that contemplates the psyche only as consciousness. Hans-Georg Gadamer, on the other hand, thinks that a person settles into prejudice because she or he is born and develops within a historical tradition. A particularly frequent way of sustaining and defending prejudices has to do with the written word ("the written word has the stability of a reference, it is like a piece of evidence", says Gadamer, and he adds: "It takes a very great critical effort to free oneself from the generalised prejudice in favour of the written word, and to distinguish ... what is opinion from what is truth").[12] For this disciple of Heidegger, prejudice is a form of knowledge of the subject, and he teaches us that, rather than closing us off from knowledge, it opens us up to the subjective world of the person issuing the prejudice – a point of view very similar to that held by psychoanalysis, for example, in relation to lies: lies reveal much more about the subject and his inner world than the subject assumes. Gadamer concludes that "an individual's prejudices are, much more than his judgements, the historical reality of his being".[13] From this perspective, we could almost coin the phrase: "tell me what your prejudices, superstitions and religion are, and I will tell you who you are".

Although the best known and most frequently mentioned prejudices are racist, social, class and religious, it is clear that virtually any issue can fall under prejudicial beliefs, including the concept of prejudice itself. For Gadamer, the revolution represented by Enlightenment thought implied, secondarily, a prejudice against prejudices, as, for this author, prejudices are a fundamental source of knowledge about the subject.

On the other hand, prejudices are emotional forms of thought close to the primary process (and, therefore, not based on experience or the judging function), related in some way to intuition and still ill-defined aspects of the perception of the inner world. In order to try to approach their understanding from a different angle, it may be useful to turn to the analysis of certain forms of popular language. When our young people speak of a *good vibe*, or of a good or bad *vibe* as a reaction to a certain person, they are describing the obscure perception of an inner reaction to the presence of the other, a preverbal form that has to do with the bodily self and with the functioning of the primary process. *Vibe* is a metaphorical – but very close to reality – way of referring to bodily vibrations, to the skin tremors and muscle tones with which we instinctively react to a fellow human being. *Bad vibes* is a linguistic way of referring to a bodily response to a subject that provokes, first, a very slight elevation of muscle tone – the function of which tends to prepare us for attack or escape – and, second, a very discrete cutaneous response of piloerection and vasoconstriction; in other words, when we speak of a *bad vibe*, we are trying to describe an attenuated and discrete form of what we know as a "general alarm reaction", a kind of discrete warning of potential danger in the presence of a stranger, the unknown other. As we can see, we are describing a mechanism of the bodily self that is an equivalent of the feeling of distress perceived by the psychic self and that prepares us for something potentially dangerous. It is important to note, however, that this type of eminently bodily and unconscious reaction has to do with the identities that, without realising it, we establish between what we perceive, in this case a certain person, and our experiential baggage; we can, therefore, say that important components of our *alarm* reaction depend more on our internal world than on objective reality.

This type of bodily process can help us to understand the elementary and primary nature of the reaction to the stranger and the unknown, as well as the possibility of grasping that this reaction to the danger that the other signifies can have a correspondence with the real characteristics of this external object – those that provoke this reaction – or, on the contrary, respond to a state of apprehension derived from a persecutory object in the internal world of the subject who feels the reaction of alarm. In the latter case, the internal persecutory object will first be split from the ego and then projected on to the other. This intrapsychic mechanism is the one that takes place in the case of ethnocentric and/or racial prejudice. Following the concepts of Enrique Pichón-Rivière and Ana Pampliega de Quiroga, "whether favourable or unfavourable, prejudice is a belief of exaggerated intensity and is associated with a category. Its function is to justify by rationalisation our behaviour in relation to these categories".[14]

It follows from the above that, in the dynamics of prejudice, the mechanisms of splitting (between the good and bad objects of the internal world), of projective identification and introjective identification (in order to place in the other the undesired, dangerous and persecutory aspects of the subject, while at the same time being able to appropriate and incorporate the admired and/or envied components of the other) are operating, as well as denial (thanks to which the perception of the parts of reality that could question or cast doubt on the rearrangements made from the dynamics of desire is avoided). The end result of this defensive constellation is similar to the manic position – described by M. Klein – whereby the persecutory inner parts of the subject are split off, denied and placed in the other. In this way, the object is denigrated and repudiated.

One of the most relevant characteristics of racist prejudice has to do, precisely, with that exaggerated emotional intensity and the rationalisation of which Enrique Pichón-Rivière and Ana Pampliega speak, the mechanism of denigration of the object – up to its reification, as could be seen in the justification of the so-called *final solution* in Nazi Germany – and with the total conviction of the subject – the aforementioned rationalization – possessing the attributes and characteristics of the good object. Being *Aryan* was synonymous with being good and just. In this way, the subject achieves the eternal narcissistic aspiration of the Ideal Self – as the race to which she or he belongs is the good, original or prototypical one – and approaches the experience of the Ideal, hedonic Self – that is, the golden Self of infantile narcissism. Hence the importance that subjects attach to emphasising what is different in the other, that the other races are only diminished and bastardised variants of the true one, which is their own, and, through this, to affirm identity, the solidity of selfhood (the *self*) and the limits of the ego in relation to the other. In contrast, when it is assumed that the other is a *similar*, the subject can enter into serious anxieties of a denominational or symbiotic nature, as she or he then feels threatened by the possibility of fusion and confusion with the other, by the diffusion of his or her identity, in Erik H. Erikson's terms.[15] Hence the need to support small differences with all our energy, a narcissism in which racist prejudice is anchored and on which it feeds, a belief in the service of separation–individuation and the possibility of autonomous affirmation in the face of the other, defined as a quasi-similar and, fortunately, different, inferior, despicable. In this way, thanks to the projection, defencelessness, anguish and castration are, finally, in the other.

We also know that prejudices can be fostered by nationalism and patriotism or, to put it better, jingoism. In an event from the not so distant past, on 31 December 1958, the Guatemalan government of Miguel Ydígoras Fuentes ordered an air strike against Mexican fishing boats that used to violate the waters of the neighbouring country, an attack that resulted in three fishermen dead and 14 wounded, and a situation of serious tension arose between the two countries (known as the Mexico–Guatemala Conflict 1958–59); in a matter of days and by virtue of the possibility of war with the neighbours, this conflict created anti-Guatemalan prejudice of serious proportions, promoted by the government and orchestrated by the media. The Mexican population, twinned for more than one reason with its southern neighbours – and hardly aware of the name of Guatemala's president beforehand – developed the most virulent of prejudices against this neighbour country, calling its president by the defamatory "*idiotígoras*" and developing, in a matter of days, an intense and irrational hatred of the once "Guatemalan brothers". However, it is also true that, after the diplomatic crisis had passed, the waters returned to their course quite quickly. It is hardly necessary to recall how easy it is for governments to manipulate their citizens to encourage or discourage prejudicial attitudes against enemy peoples or minorities in their own population.

A clear example from the recent past, illustrative of the possibilities of stimulating and revealing latent racial prejudice, is Proposition 187, with which the former governor Pete Wilson manipulated Californians in order to make the so-called illegal immigrants bear full responsibility for the labour and financial crisis in the State of California in the 1990s. In fact, a clear demonstration that this was manipulation of society for strictly electoral purposes could be seen in the fact that the same person, when he was a senator, had fought for the establishment of laws that had a broad tolerance for illegal migration because, at that time, these laws helped landowners and industrialists who, in this way, could mercilessly exploit these workers by paying them wages far below what the law established and easily make extra profits. We can see how the potential of racial prejudice was the same in 1994 as before; it was just used for different purposes. Just as, in the beginning, Pete Wilson had no qualms about receiving substantial "gifts" from the powerful tycoons he benefited, in order to justify the denigration of illegal immigrants by subjecting them to a form of slave labour, now the same person received help and attractive gifts to apply racism for another purpose: to create a scapegoat on which society could project all that was wrong in California. As we can see, the Americans employed the same tactics as Hitler's Germany did, with the same economic determinants at the time.[16]

Repetition of the labour and economic crisis in our northern neighbours also repeats the *appearance* of racist prejudice, but now promoted by the Republican governor, Jan Brewer, in the State of Arizona where, in 2010, in a pseudo-legalistic justification (what we know as rationalisation), she passed a law (SB-1070) against the previously accepted – and exploited – migrant workers. It was a law seconded, with modifications, by the states of Alabama, Georgia, Indiana, South Carolina and Utah. The purported legal arguments, in reality, cover up the promotion of anti-immigrant prejudice, as clearly shown by Joe Arpaio, the sheriff of Maricopa County, whose actions – to the point of cruelty and with total lack of empathy for the shattered lives, separated families and deportation of people who had dedicated their entire lives to the productivity of the state – have won the admiration of the most backward US Republicans.

What kind of psychological and social levers were mobilised by the political advisors of the governors of California, Arizona and other US states in order to channel the potential for anti-Latin American prejudice in general and anti-Mexican prejudice in particular among the citizens of those states? As was the case with the Jews in Nazi Germany, the scapegoat dynamic is one of the most popular tools when there is a socio-economic crisis in a state. Ever since the Bible, we have known that the function of the scapegoat is to take the blame for an unfavourable social situation and pay the price. In the brief cases of California and Arizona, the illegal Hispanic minority has been blamed for economic hardship. The propaganda of these Republican governors had the effect of channelling popular citizen discontent towards illegal migrants by making them appear to be the cause of huge, unnecessary public spending on health care and education budgets. The spurious pretext of potentially cost-saving state spending could only be sustained through the blatant denial of other opposing factors in boom times, when "wetbacks" were encouraged to migrate to work in the fields or in jobs that Americans did not want for themselves. It is common knowledge that this group of undocumented migrants has had a strong positive influence on agriculture and industry and, in general, on the region's economy; this does not invalidate their foreignness, their physical and cultural differences, language, eating habits and other issues. These differences, when the situation may require it, contribute to racially and culturally based prejudice.

As we can see, prejudices can be manipulated for political, financial or electoral purposes (a particularly transparent example from the recent past is Donald Trump's use of such anti-Mexican prejudices). However, we should not forget that the vast majority of prejudices are inculcated by family and culture, and so, if Jews are seen as bad or dangerous in our family and social group, we will tend to aprioristically view them that way. If, on the other hand, we are born into a Jewish environment in which gentiles are viewed with suspicion and as potentially threatening people, then we will develop a similar prejudiced view.

Another example is the notorious neo-Nazi *skinhead* movement, which began in response to the labour crisis that followed the fall of the symbolic Berlin Wall and German unification, when workers in the former East Germany were caught in a severe unemployment crisis. Social discontent, anchored in an ideological pseudo-justification inspired by racist prejudice, manifested itself as people began to fight to take back the jobs that Turks, North Africans and other foreigners had been doing in the country, having migrated when West Germany urgently needed and favoured labour to carry out its economic recovery after peace was achieved at the end of the Second World War. Again, we see how rationalisation can negate what is, strictly speaking, a racist prejudice, now against Turks, black North Africans and other foreigners.

Finally, and to integrate what is happening in my own country, in Mexico we can observe various forms of prejudice, both racial and ethnocentric. In this way, what once applied to Guatemalans has also prevailed, at different times and owing to different circumstances, in the prejudices against *gachupines* and *Frenchies* or *gabachos*, *gringos*, Jews, blacks and *chales* with slanted eyes, all terms that contain ideas of prejudice against Spaniards, French, Americans, East Asians of all kinds and so on. However, one of its most conspicuous manifestations is the racial denigration of indigenous ethnicities and all things indigenous in general. The denigration of the object contained in the way the *pinches indios* – as they are often called, plainly and simply – or *nacos* – in the softened but equally denigrating version – are rejected has to do with old difficulties in assuming the indigenous part within the two main ethnic elements from which Mexican identity has been shaped.

Prejudice can, therefore, occur in the psyche of the subject, but also in the imaginary of peoples; it is as much an element of the individual mentality as it is of the collective unconscious of communities.

One more example of prejudice-based thinking has to do with the very recent belief – which originated in Mexico, but permeated the world through the mass media – that the world would end on 21 December 2012. This mythical construction was a prejudgement as it was uncritically based on a misrepresentation of Mayan codices announcing the end of *baktun* 12 on 20 December and the beginning of *baktun* 13 on 21 December, but adding the fact – lacking any real support – that this meant the end of the world. No matter how many times the falsity of this erroneous interpretation of the codices appeared in the media, there was a tendency to believe that these *ancient and sacred* Mayan documents of *ancient and sacred wisdom* foretold the end of time on that day. It is quite possible that the combination of the change of *baktun* and the fact that *baktun* 13 began – an ominous number par excellence – contributed to this distorted and almost delirious interpretation of the texts and gave rise to magical thinking, totally dissociated from what the codices actually say but attached to certain needs of the unconscious collective imagination. This type of construction is not accidental, as we know of a great multiplicity of precedents in which humanity has believed that the world was going to end. The penultimate episode of this occurred when the year 2000 was reached, which, from the magic granted to round numbers, brought about a wave of panic on a global scale, as also happened when humanity faced the year 1000.[17] In this case, we can see the need to cling to a thought that is alien to the judgement of reality – prejudgement, superstition or delirium anchored in magical forms of thought – in order to give way to one of the most fundamental terrors of human beings: the fear of death and its historical-genetic determinant in the defencelessness with which the infant is born.

We speak of racist prejudice when a person or community maintains an attitude of negative valence towards another subject or group, an emotional attitude sustained a priori in the knowledge of that individual or group and based on the physical characteristics of the subject or group discriminated against.[18] In these cases, physical attributes that have to do with skin colour and physiognomic features are considered, without any causal reasoning, as determinants of the forms of social behaviour and of certain moral or intellectual qualities of these subjects. Racism is, therefore, in principle, a prejudice refractory to experience and tends to perpetuate itself on the basis of values inculcated during childhood that form part of the ideology with which a given subject is born and grows up in a family and a specific society. Attitudes of racist animosity thus constitute one more ingredient of the culture transmitted from parents to children in the chain of generations.

As we can see, racial prejudice refers to psychic representations that have become cathected by intense negative and irrational affections, strongly rooted in the family and social ideology introjected and incorporated into the unconscious part of the ego and the superego (where the Ideal of the Ego is not alien) from the earliest childhood, present in a latent form in all human beings but able to be actualised under historical or political circumstances that stimulate them and are capable of triggering and channelling them in a specific direction and towards specific population groups – frequently towards minority communities. For Nathan W. Ackerman and Marie Jahoda, who have attempted to study the specificity of anti-Semitism (albeit with little success), "the person raised in an anti-Semitic environment, who has never seen a Jew, and who was taught in Sunday school that *the Jews killed Christ*, is most likely to assume a hostile attitude towards Jews".[19]

These negative emotions provoke all kinds of behavioural manifestations, some of which may be more or less aggressive, and the repercussions or consequences of which are felt in the social or political–economic field. The result of this type of manipulation is a social behaviour of clear animosity towards the discriminated group.

Ackerman and Jahoda define racial prejudice as "an attitude of hostility in interpersonal relations, directed against an entire group or individuals belonging to it, and filling a definite irrational function within the personality".[20] For these authors, prejudice-dominated personalities often exhibit a certain rigidity and aversion to the exercise of introspection. They also distinguish between prejudiced thoughts and stereotyped ways of thinking, as a distinction must be made between prejudice that occurs when facts are not at hand, and, therefore, thinking is limited by an incomplete experience of them, and stereotyped thinking in which facts do not count, even if they are at hand. The distinction drawn by Ackerman and Jahoda is interesting, as it is very different from a type of thinking that does not benefit from knowledge, from one that persists despite the data provided by perception and knowledge of the facts. In this way, prejudice and stereotypical thinking are two close modalities of the same process that has to do with beliefs. On the other hand, James Parkes agrees with other scholars of the phenomenon and asserts that prejudices make use, primarily, of three mental mechanisms: projection, displacement and rationalisation.[21]

It should be made clear that, when we speak of racial prejudice, we are referring to a type of discrimination based on race – an ambiguous term that is difficult to define. In general, we tend to speak of race only in the broadest sense of the term – that is, when we make the classic distinction between the three great human groups: the so-called yellow, white and black races, as the so-called copper race (or the very Mexican bronze race) corresponds to a subclassification of the previous ones. Any other attempt to classify human groups on the basis of racial determinants encounters insurmountable difficulties. In fact, the arguments put forward by certain nations in search of distinctive attributes from the concept of race – as is the case with the defenders of the so-called Aryan race – are much more related to family and/or ideological introjects of a racist type than to defining arguments based on empirical reality data that could, eventually, allow for a reasonable classification.

What caused the human species to be circumscribed to these three major modalities of *Homo sapiens*? We do not know, but it is obvious that climate and other environmental determinants, as well as the conditions of forced inbreeding brought about by geographical barriers at the dawn of humanity, contributed to the creation of characteristics that later became distinctive in human groups with different physical traits from one another. But it would be interesting to explore and highlight the multiple causes from which the linguistic definitions given to these human groups were structured. I do not think it is accidental that colour-related parameters have been chosen to mark the physical differences between the three human groups. White, black and yellow are colours that undoubtedly, beyond the support that the colour of the integument provided at the time, have some kind of emotional significance.

It should be noted that colours are one of the closest and most direct forms for the expression of affect. These derivatives of drive escape the need for word-representation – which is why they enter consciousness as thing-representations, without the customary processing of the word in the preconscious – and are made metaphors through colours (as occurs with the artistic manifestations of the plastic arts) or sounds (as occurs in the case of music). We know that colour, sound, movement and space are forms or attempts – more successful than the written or spoken word – to transmit or make known those emotional states that the word can barely stammer out. Painting, music, dance, sculpture and archi-tecture are privileged means of connecting perception with the inner world of emotion. Black, white and yellow are the expression of emotional states, and it is clear that they are not only descriptions of physical characteristics, except for their weak support in the integument.

On the other hand, it is quite obvious that, in physiognomic, bodily and integument descriptions, ideology cannot but be present. In our Western cul-tures, when we speak of the thick lips and frizzy hair of black people or the slanting eyes of yellow people, we do so from the ideological model that has been the paradigm of our aesthetic canons; that is, our descriptions are based on the ideals of beauty of Greco-Roman culture, as these physical attributes and physiognomic features are described in comparison and contrast with the so-called white race, particularly that modality that occurred in classical Greece and in republican and imperial Rome. Thus, we understand that the lips of black people are *thicker* than those of white people, and the eyes of yellow people are oblique *in comparison* with those of white people. Similar parameters define the smallness of the Pygmies, the height of the Hottentots, the blackness of the Ethiopians, the thinness of the Chinese, the high cheek-bones of the Slavs or the bony characteristics of the Australians.

We do not yet know the origin and concrete forms of the link between a colour and certain emotions. We know of the attraction and interest, con-stitutionally given, that red and yellow exert on the infants of the human species; of the sedative characteristics of green; of the whiteness by which goodness, kindness and purity are defined (despite the fact that white is formed by the mixture of all colours); the identification of black – the absence of light – with night and, by extension, with dangerous situations, with evil, sinisterness and death; the action of yellow as a stimulant of the cerebral cortex; and so on. As we can see, the colours and the races behind them very possibly also have to do with affects that have been induced to serve as ideational representatives in function of cultural elements learned and transmitted generationally, although anchored in neurophysiological factors of a constitutional nature. Colours provoke primitive feelings in the bodily "I", although we are hardly able to describe the sensations they provoke. We also sense that this is a very basic level of integration, prior to any possibility of conceptualising the experience.

As we can see from the above, it follows, once again, that the potential to exhibit prejudiced attitudes is in all of us and constitutes an unavoidable element of our cultural baggage. The importance of the study of racial prejudice has to do with the fact that these are emotional attitudes towards members of rival exo-groups, neighbouring peoples or communities from which we have to differentiate ourselves somewhat forcibly because they stem from a common trunk – prejudices whose roots are located in deep, unconscious strata of our psyche. They are affective attitudes that are completely irrational and disconnected from any logical consideration or reasoning on the part of the secondary process, hardly modifiable by reality or experience, but susceptible to being manipulated, stimulated or directed in a particular direction according to various interests: for political reasons, in order to create intragroup cohesion; in the context of war, as an element justifying expansionist national movements; to carry out a war operation to protect sovereignty; or for religious reasons, when it serves as a stimulus to carry out holy wars.

Superstition

We can define superstitions as those irrational beliefs (contrary to reason) about things and their causes, events or dates that, as a result of a conceptual treatment stemming from magical thinking, are dangerous or ominous. Strictly speaking, the superstitious way of understanding things derives from a prejudiced way of processing perception and information, and, therefore, superstition is a cognitive – and emotional – form of prejudice; it is a form of cognitive distortion in our perception of reality, a distortion anchored in the principle of authority (what our elders instilled in us during childhood, which is the form of generational transmission of prejudices and superstitions) and in determinants of our unconscious inner world. From this perspective, superstition is only separated by a tenuous line from what are normal perceptual processes that, out of necessity, always involve a certain distortion of reality: it is a quantitative rather than a qualitative distinction. Even for some researchers in human psychology, our psyche has a natural tendency towards a superstitious processing of reality. An example is the affective appreciation we may have for certain objects – the suit we get married in, certain photographs, the song that defines a couple's relationship, the pen with which a poem, novel or scientific paper was written and so on. Many people are convinced that keeping pesos, dollars and euros in their pocket on New Year's Eve will bring good luck for their finances in the year ahead, as well as wearing red underwear being a good omen for love and other customs that, without possessing the systematisation of superstitions – the number 13, black cats and so on – are very close in their aetiology and dynamics to them.

It was only after its redefinition by the great figures of the Catholic Church that superstition began to be explained and related to religions, and, since then, it is usually defined as a "belief foreign to religious faith and contrary to reason".[22] In the Catholic version, superstition would be any religion or form of faith other than that of that religion; even that which has to do with the devil is described as superstitious.

Thanks to the magical thinking that underlies all superstitions, incantations, spells, prayers, rituals and various forms of incantations can be established in order to avert danger or potential harm from the object or situation that the superstition has identified as threatening or ominous – which brings them closer to religions. From the superstitious perspective, there are causal relationships between everyday events and forces understood as supernatural, and, hence, the aetiology of these phenomena has to do with such deleterious aspects as fate, the influence of the stars on the behaviour and history of human beings, the world of magic and rituals, or the power of the dead and the spirit world over the lives of the living.

Walking under a ladder on a Tuesday – or Friday – the 13th ("On a Tuesday thirteenth neither marry nor embark nor leave your family", goes a popular saying);[23] a black cat crossing our path; breaking a mirror and its 7-year period of bad luck; starting the day on the wrong foot; opening an umbrella inside the house; the evil eye and its various remedies; buying lottery tickets from a hunchback or finding a four-leaf clover; spilling salt or wine on the table; knocking on wood or crossing your fingers; carrying a rabbit's foot in your pocket or taking the precaution of hanging a horseshoe behind the door; and a very long list of etceteras – including the superstition and curse against those who explored Tutankhamun's tomb; putting cacti on windows and doors; the paraphernalia of feng shui; the belief that a bride has to wear something old, something borrowed, something new and something blue; throwing coins backwards into a fountain or well – these are some of the most common superstitions in our civilisations, both Eastern and Western.

For example, the custom that it is good luck to put cacti on the windows and doors of a house comes from an ancient tradition that cacti keep evil away from houses because of their ability to absorb moisture from the environment. Their protective effect derives from the fact that evil spirits need moisture to thrive and thus do not prosper owing to the preventive function of cacti. This is a theory that predates the Hippocratic era and the theses on humidity or dryness of humours, mixed with concepts from old Asian and European demonologies. Similarly, the Jewish Cabala lists 13 evil spirits, and, in the Tarot, 13 is the number linked to death. In some cultures, the number 13 is said to come from the Last Supper of the Christian tradition, with Jesus Christ and the 12 apostles. According to this, when there are 13 at a table, in the course of that year one of the guests will die. The association of 13 with Tuesday comes from Roman tradition, as that day was dedicated to Mars, the god of war and violence, hence its ominous combination. Christian tradition also interprets touching wood as having to do with the cross on which Christ died; however, there are testimonies from 4,000 years ago that attribute its beneficial effects to the custom of veneration of the oak tree as the dwelling place of the gods, as well as for being a maternal symbol of protection against danger.

The problem is that superstitions are very difficult to eradicate, and the possibility of people abandoning these types of beliefs based on superstitious prejudices is very problematic owing to their origins in the deep layers of the unconscious, their generational transmission together with the rest of the elements of the culture in which the subject is born and grows up, and the fact that they have a very economic role in psychic functioning. It is important to note that many of these superstitious prejudices go back to remote epochs of our civilisation, stages in which pre-scientific thinking of a magical or religious type still predominated, and, therefore, they have to do with a form of mental functioning determined by the primary process. Superstitions are a form of mental functioning in which the subject is unconsciously convinced that she or he can control the world and the events that occur in it. Admitting that chance governs the external world is very distressing because it leaves us unprotected and helpless in the face of its contingencies, hence the need, through magical thinking, to establish rules governing that world and special manoeuvres to control it – prayers, psalms, rites of all kinds. The establishment of beliefs and taboos allows us to know the causalities that govern such events and a way to protect ourselves or to regulate, to some extent, their influence.

Religious Systems

Religions are constituted as organised and more or less coherent sets of prejudices, superstitions, taboos and rituals with strong magical thinking content. Although this statement may seem too strong or reckless, we think that Freud was right when he said that religions are delusional systems of thought.[24] Let us even recall that, as early as 1907, he defined the characteristics of the obsessive-compulsive neurotic as being immersed in a kind of private religion, whereas religions can be seen as systems of obsessive ritualisation of humanity.[25] And, just as the obsessive does not question the significance of the rituals that chain him or her to a restricted and miserable life, neither does the religious person question the significance of ceremonials, however restrictive they may be to his or her personal freedom. In both cases, reason is replaced by belief or dogma – that is, by a prejudgement or superstition, where there is no room for critical thinking.

What is interesting is that we find religious systems in all cultures and for as long as we have historical memory – and even earlier if we take into account the data provided by prehistoric finds – which tells us of the need for belief, independent of knowledge. At the dawn of humanity, primitive human beings, surrounded by a nature they did not understand, survived through mistrust and fear. Their existence was determined by their ability to antici- pate, to foresee dangers before they became present; hence the need to focus their intelligence with a defensive orientation. However, it is clear that some of these dangers, some of the potentially persecutory features of nature, were nothing more than projections into the world of their nascent psyche. Thus was born what we know as the animistic stage of primitive thought. Light- ning and cloud, water and rain, sun and moon, animals, trees and rocks, everything was endowed with a spirit; all things, organic and inorganic, pulsed with life and possessed a soul. To the animistic mind, the whole cosmos was interrelated and concerted like a great universal symphony. This early, animistic way of thinking of primitive human beings is the origin of the concept of the spirit that inhabited all things, including humans themselves, who were thus thought of as endowed with a soul. Animism is related to prehistoric people's inability to distinguish the material from the immaterial, the animate from the inanimate world, the visible, tangible and audible world that their sense organs informed them of from their own inner, invisible, phantasmatic world, full of mental representations, affections and chains of thoughts. The greatest evolutionary leap was represented by the acquisition of words to name both the things and events of the external world and the affective states of their inner world. The development of language, through which they began to associate images with situations and affects, slowly shaped languages and, with them, human communication.

In the course of evolution, a primitive human was able to establish certain boundaries, such as the distinction between his or her "I" and his or her "not- I", which began to be understood as the surrounding world. He or she assumed that even others, although they were his or her fellows, were not part of his or her "I". At the same time, he or she became aware of living in a universe governed by time and realised with increasing subtlety the distinction between what happened in the past and the present, between memory and perception. This awareness of a past marked the beginning of a historical conception of a human, on the outside, as well as a growing awareness of his or her identity as a subject, on the inside. This progressive awareness of the notion of temporality would gradually mark humans' most transcendental acquisition, for it confronted them with a fact from which they have not yet recovered: they became aware of the phenomenon of death. The empirical and everyday realisation that all living beings die includes humans them- selves: human beings can die and can kill. An individual's realisation that many of the old people he or she knew have already died and are left behind, in the past, makes him or her understand a new and final dimension of time: the future. In this way, he or she becomes aware that he or she too will die in a near or remote but unavoidable future. He or she realises that there are phenomena and events determined by laws that are beyond humans and their pretensions of control. Human beings are governed by regulations similar to those that cause day and night, the phases of the moon and the tides, agricultural cycles and the seasons of the year.

From these observations, humans soon came to believe that the entire universe – and their own lives – was governed by suprahuman, immortal, all-powerful deities, embodied from the earliest times in the forces of nature: the sun, the moon, the ocean, the earth and so on. At the same time, it endowed these deities with the same desires, passions, hatreds and pleasures as human beings themselves. These notions gave rise to the first rudiments of religion.[26]

The next step had to do with the need to communicate with these deities: as the gods determine the course and vicissitudes of human lives, incantations, prayers and rites become necessary elements for communication with the gods, for making transactions with them. This is how what we know as religions were structured; as we can see, they were based on more or less fantasised or magical beliefs, without any support in the data of reality. In turn, the priests – who eventually became the priestly class – would soon be people endowed with *special attributes* that made them the specialists and intermediaries in dealing with the deities. A very important part of the thinking behind religion is that religion becomes the best instrument for handling the hurtful uncertainty about our most fundamental questions of who we are, where we come from and where we are going. Religions, claiming to be in possession of the ability to answer such questions, produced the first religious dogmas, based on beliefs and fantasies, but, thanks to them, human beings could feel protected and guarded by higher entities that watched over them in their misfortune, in the same way that small children feel cared for by their parents.

As the projection of the inner world was systematised in perfectly characterised gods, these could also be objects of worship, veneration and sacred fear, but at the same time they were deities susceptible to listening to mortals' reasons, their sorrows and supplications, to be appeased with prayers and psalms, with various sacrificial rites and offerings, they could even be bought and blackmailed with various manoeuvres in which they were obliged to follow a certain conduct.

Religious thought was a very important step forward in relation to the previous animistic phase. As Erich Kahler has shown us, when one moves from the animistic state of participation with the universal whole to a stage of objectification, religion is born, the starting point of which has to do with the establishment of worship and cult. Worship is the specific form of human communication with these deified entities projected into a superhuman world.[27]

One of the constitutive characteristics of human beings has to do with an innate curiosity and an irreducible need to know: let us remember that the sin of Adam and Eve, according to the myth, derived from their curiosity and greed for knowledge, and this proved to have much more motivational force and importance than the tendency to tranquillity and placidity offered by the earthly paradise of a life devoted to idleness and laziness. Human beings want to know where they come from, where they are and where they are going. Moreover, the hominid from which we evolved has an almost non-existent tolerance for uncertainty, hence the need to find an explanation for everything, even that which has no explanation. Humans want to know the cause of the universe they inhabit, even though it is possible that the cosmos has no such primordial cause. They need to explain to themselves what happens and why it happens, even if it has no semblance of a metaphysical purpose. What is the meaning of a life that has been given to us without our participation, but which we have to deal with every day of our existence? It would seem that we are so intolerant of such questions and uncertainties that we stubbornly resist imagining that the universe, as we know it, has no hidden causes, purposes or meanings, hence the need to construct religious systems in which such uncertainties are answered and resolved, and which offer explanations – sometimes very close to fictional literature – regardless of whether such assertions can be sustained from the perspective of logic or scientific knowledge. What is important is that religions exercise a reassuring effect on human beings by providing them with various forms of theogonies that are perfectly articulated and coherent, except in one point: their basis of support. In this way, religions and their systems of thought are indistinguishable from delusions: coherent and perfectly articulated, except in their starting points, which are false or unprovable.

As we can see, religions, like superstitions, are based on judgements formulated a priori and disconnected from any kind of evidence. In fact, the distinction between religious and scientific thinking is that the latter is subject to constant revision and possibility of falsification – that is, it is modifiable by virtue of advances in knowledge and has ruled out the possibility of absolute truths – whereas religious thought is based on immutable and unquestionable dogmas, on absolute truths, making it impossible to carry out any kind of criticism or possibility of ratification or rectification of them.

As we said at the beginning, there is a great distance between what constitutes a belief – a prejudice, superstition, religious system – and what we understand as knowledge, always being questioned and expanded, based on transitory truths. Prejudice, superstition and the delusions that underlie religious systems are processes that, by not taking into account the data provided by reality, we can understand as being closer to desire, to the pleasure principle and to the primary process. In contrast, knowledge is strongly anchored in the reality principle, critical thinking and the secondary process.

Notes

1 Sigmund Freud (1915–1916, 1916–1917): 2123–2412.
2 Albert Camus (1942).
3 Hanna Segal (1964).
4 Louis Althusser (1970).
5 Fanny Blanck-Cereijido (2009).
6 S. Freud (1895): 237.
7 Ibid., p. 238.
8 René Spitz (1965).
9 S. Freud (1925).
10 Diccionario Enciclopédico Salvat Universal (1971a).
11 José Ferrater Mora (1979): 2672.
12 Hans-Georg Gadamer (1975): 339.
13 Ibid., p. 344.
14 Enrique Pichón-Ricière and Ana Pampliega de Quiroga (1970): 145.
15 Erik H. Erikson (1950).
16 Juan Vives (1994).
17 Georges Duby (1967).
18 J. Vives (1995).
19 Nathan W. Ackerman and Marie Jahoda (1950): 28.
20 Ibid., p. 25.
21 James Parkes (1963).
22 *Diccionario Enciclopédico Salvat Universal* (1971b).
23 Not only do many hotels and buildings omit the 13th floor, but, since the Babylo-
    nian King Hammurabi's Code, the number 13 has been omitted from the compi-
    lation of laws because it was considered to be a bad omen. The reaction against
    the number 13 can become so intense that it eventually takes the clinical form of a
    real phobia, so-called triskaidekaphobia – an inordinate terror of the number 13,
    which, by the way, is the seventh prime number, seven being a magical number
    with a centuries-old tradition dating back to the culture of Ancient Egypt.
24 S. Freud (1927).
25 S. Freud (1907).
26 J. Vives (1997).
27 Erich Kahler (1943).

References

Ackerman, N.W. and Jahoda, M. (1950): *Psicoanálisis del antisemitismo* (Psychoanalysis of anti-Semitism), trans. by Julio Garber, Buenos Aires, Ed. Paidós (2nd
ed., 1962).
Althusser, L. (1970): "Ideology and ideological apparatuses of the state (Notes for an
investigation)", in *Philosophy as a Weapon of Revolution*, trans. by Oscar del Barco,
Enrique Román and Oscar I. Molina. Mexico, Cuadernos de Pasado y Presente
(9th ed., 1979), pp. 97–141.
Blanck-Cereijido, F. (2009): "Prejuicio, intolerancia y odio al otro" (Prejudice, intolerance
and hatred of the other), *Revista de Psicoanálisis de Guadalajara* (Mexico), 4: 65–74.
Camus, A. (1942): *The Foreigner*, trans. by Bonifacio del Carril, Mexico, Ed. Promesa,
1979.
Diccionario Enciclopédico Salvat Universal(1971a): Prejudice, vol. 10, Barcelona,
Salvat Ed., p. 2745.

Diccionario Enciclopédico Salvat Universal (1971b): Superstition, vol. 12, Barcelona, Salvat Ed., p. 3113.

Duby, G. (1967): *El año mil* (The year one thousand), trans. by Irene Agoff, Barcelona, Ed. Gedisa, 1996.

Erikson, E.H. (1950): *Infancia y sociedad* (Childhood and society), trans. by Noemí Rosenblatt, Buenos Aires, Ed. Hormé, 3rd ed., 1970.

Ferrater Mora, J. (1979): *Diccionario de Filosofía* (Dictionary of philosophy), vol. 3, Madrid, Alianza Editorial.

Freud, S. (1895): "Project of a psychology for neurologists", in *Obras completes* (Complete works), vol. II, trans. by Luis López-Ballesteros, Madrid, Biblioteca Nueva, 3rd ed.

Freud, S. (1907): "Obsessive acts and religious practices", in *Obras completes* (Complete works), vol. II, trans. by Luis López-Ballesteros, Madrid, Biblioteca Nueva, 3rd ed, pp. 1337–1342.

Freud, S. (1915–1916, 1916–1917): "Introductory lessons in psychoanalysis", in *Obras completes* (Complete works), vol. II, trans. by Luis López-Ballesteros, Madrid, Biblioteca Nueva, 3rd ed, pp. 2123–2412.

Freud, S. (1925): "The negation", in *Obras completes* (Complete works), vol. II, trans. by Luis López-Ballesteros, Madrid, Biblioteca Nueva, 3rd ed, pp. 2884–2886.

Freud, S. (1927): "The future of an illusion", in *Obras completes* (Complete works), vol. III, trans. by Luis López-Ballesteros, Madrid, Biblioteca Nueva, 3rd ed, pp. 2961–2992.

Gadamer, H.-G. (1975): *Verdad y método I. Fundamentos de una hermenéutica filosófica* (Truth and method I: Foundations of a philosophical hermeneutics), trans. by Ana Agud Aparicio and Rafael de Agapito, Salamanca, Ed. Sígueme, 6th ed., 1996.

Kahler, E. (1943): *Historia Universal del Hombre* (Universal history of man), trans. by Javier Márquez, Mexico, Fondo de Cultura Económica, 4th ed., 1965.

Parkes, J. (1963): *Antisemitismo* (Antisemitism), trans. by Nelly R. de Sarli, Buenos Aires, Ed. Paidós, 1965.

Pichón-Rivière, E. and Pampliega de Quiroga, A. (1970): *Psicología de la vida cotidiana* (Psychology of everyday life), Buenos Aires.

Segal, H. (1964): *Introduction to the work of Melanie Klein*, trans. by Hebe Friedenthal, Buenos Aires, Ed. Paidós, 1970.

Spitz, R. (1965): *El primer año de vida del niño* (The first year of the child's life), trans. by Manuel de la Escalera, Mexico, Fondo de Cultura Económica, 1969.

Vives, J. (1994): "Motivos y consecuencias de la Propuesta 187" (Motives and consequences of Proposition 187), *Página Uno* (supplement to *Unomásuno*), No. 688, 11 December, p. 14.

Vives, J. (1995): "El prejuicio racial" (Racial prejudice), *Jornada Psicoanalítica* (Guadalajara), 11: 47–59.

Vives, J. (1997): "La religión como sistema delirante" (Religion as a delusional system), paper read as part of the Symposium "Psicoanálisis y Religión" (Psychoanalysis and religion), held at the Mexican Psychoanalytic Association, Mexico City, 12 July 1997.

Chapter 2

Prejudice and Racism

Olivia Gall

Evolutionary Biological and Identity Pressures: The Origin of the Construction of Otherness as Threatening and Inferior

It is quite clear that one of the most common tendencies among groups of the human species is to categorise people. This arises, it is thought, from a fundamental evolutionary pressure, stemming from the fact that we need to distinguish friends from enemies. In this context,

> friends can be defined as those who can extend our own genetic viability. [...] Adversaries, by contrast, are those who undermine, endanger, inhibit or attack our well-being and the well-being of those who are genetically connected to us. Therefore, there is good reason to distinguish people on the basis of whether they are on our side or against us, whether they are from our group or from another group, whether they are friends or rivals.
>
> (Jones, 1996: 204)

But, in addition to that dimension of evolutionary pressure that leads us to defend our biological existence and the natural habitat in which it develops, there is another dimension of this same pressure, identity pressure, which is just as powerful as the first. Human beings have lived in groups since we were born as a species on this planet. These range from the family to the national society or the union of nations – the European Union, for example – through the clan, the tribe, the ethnic group and, in more urban contexts, a multiplicity of groupings that are made up of people with whom each of us identifies for different reasons.

Since our origins as a species, which we now know to have taken place on the African continent, each group of human beings has invested an enormous amount of time and energy in reproducing, in seeking food sources, in seeking shelter from the natural elements, in ensuring that their offspring survive biologically and over time. Alongside this, each group has also invested a great deal in trying to understand its own existence and the origins and meaning of its existence – who they are, what makes them who they are, where the group comes from, and where it is going – and in endowing its

DOI: 10.4324/9781003291978-3

daily life with rituals and customs that honour and nurture the ways in which the members of such a group answer these questions.

To this end, each human group has developed a multiplicity of social, cultural, psychological and institutional tools that enable it to rely on a dimension of human life that is as fundamental as material life itself: the building of identity.

In the beginning, there were human times without history (Clastres, 1974) – that is, times inhabited by human groups that did not leave us a record of their passage on Earth. These are also called mythical times (a word the etymology of which means "logically first"), during which, for each group, it was a matter of understanding, first of all, where they came from, who they were, what powers determined life and death; of trying to deal, using these explanatory tools, with human smallness in the face of the powerful natural elements; of trying to survive and ensure their group reproduction in the future.

Each group, closed in on itself and its questions and answers, was creating in those immemorial times its initial cosmovision, its mythological corpus inhabited by its own deities, which made it feel more secure, more protected, possessing greater clarity about its existence and destiny.

To accompany this process, it went about creating culture, defined by Kroeber and Kluckhohn as

> standardised ways of thinking, feeling and reacting, acquired and transmitted mainly through symbols, which constitute a distinctive achievement of human groups, including their translation into the manufacture of artefacts. The essential core of culture consists of traditional (i.e. historically derived and selected) ideas, and especially their attached values. Cultural systems can, on the one hand, be seen as products of action and, on the other hand, as constitutive elements of future actions.
> (Kroeber and Kluckhohn, 1952: 181)

That culture, with its customs and rituals, honoured, nurtured and reproduced that world-view, which was an integral and fundamental part of it. Although elementary at the time, such cultural "tools" of human life have characterised all forms of human society as we know them today. They live and operate in the dimension of symbolic representations of group or social reality (Hardwick, 1977). Each group gradually constructs a series of symbols – mechanisms of communication between its members – that allow it to structure a corpus that is not only explanatory but also ritual, which gives collective meaning and common coherence to its very existence and to the forms it adopts.

These original human societies, like all those that have followed them, were creating, in parallel, institutions – even if they were very elementary at the beginning – ensuring that these customs and rituals were regulated, and that these rules were enforced, so that their identity edifice would continue to give meaning to their collective life and feed back into it in the form of everyday symbolic acts (Wilson, 2012: 1).

In order to construct this corpus, it was not only necessary for each group to bring together the individualities that made it up, the individual identities and personalities that, added together and combined, inhabited it, but it had to seek, within its environment and within the universe of collective perceptions that it was shaping about this environment, living beings and natural elements with which to compare itself. Only the comparison with those who are different – the Other – can allow the group, when looking at itself and the Other in a mirror, to observe that the image that the mirror returns of that or those "other/s" is not the same as that which it returns of its own material or symbolic body (Lacan, 1966).

But, in that phase of human history, the others, the different ones, existed mainly in the form of insects, animals, plants, fish, and deities considered supra-human, divine. Humans lived basically in small, nomadic, gathering clans, whose life took place in a natural habitat that, at most, covered a few hundred square kilometres.

In the historical phase immediately after this, human groups began to encounter, at some point in their evolutionary biological and identity-driven wanderings, other human groups carrying their own wanderings in these two dimensions.

When they met, each of them had to discern, in the mirror images of the two, what elements made them similar and what elements made them different. As similarities, they should in principle be able to register, to perceive, that in their biological morphological conformation these others were more similar to them than a lion, an elephant, an iguana, a palm tree or even a monkey or other primate.

But what are essential for the subject at hand are the elements in which they registered, perceived, the differences. These included, importantly, those of a cultural nature – language, kinship relations, gender relations, daily rituals around food, dress, festivals, worship of divinities – and those of an institutional nature, discussed above, both of which are central to the comparison between self-identity and the identity of others.

Identity is

> the collective perception of a relatively homogeneous "us" (*the group seen from the inside*), as opposed to "the others" (*the group from the outside*), based on the recognition of shared characters, marks and traits that also function as signs and emblems, as well as a common collective memory.
>
> (Fossaert, 1983)

One of the central factors in the analysis of the perception and recognition by human groups of the differences in identity between themselves and the other (s) they encounter is the most frequent reactions to the Other throughout history. It seems impossible to deny that, parallel to possible reactions of curiosity, attempts at rapprochement, encouragement of communication and hospitality, one of the most frequent animal reactions – humans included – to an encounter with otherness is fear of his or her differentiated identity.

The mere existence of collective otherness makes us feel threatened by the very construction of our own identity, which has not been easy to put together. We fear that our identity will be questioned, disproved or even destroyed by that of the other; that we will be left unprotected in terms of identity, at the mercy of not understanding, of not being able to explain ourselves well, of a collective life devoid of the meaning that we have given it, which, we are convinced, is the true meaning.

Therefore, once otherness appears on our horizon, we tend to fear it and reject it, to see it as incorrect, false, negative. We thus imprint on it a connotation of value, in comparison with that which we imprint on our own identity. In this regard, C. Castoriadis affirms that each of the groups that have had an encounter has three possibilities: to consider the other as superior, to consider it as equal or equivalent, or to consider it as inferior.

> We note immediately that the first case would imply both a logical contradiction and a real suicide. The consideration of "foreign" institutions as superior by the institution of a society (not by this or that individual) does not make sense: this institution would have to give way to the other.
>
> (Castoriadis, 2001: 21)[1]

The encounter, therefore, leaves only two possibilities. Castoriadis adds:

> either the others are inferior or they are equal to us. Experience shows that the first way is almost always followed and the second way almost never. There is an apparent "reason" for this. To say that others are "equal to us" could not mean equal in undifferentiation: it would imply [...] that everything would then become indifferent [in one's habits] and would cease to be done.
>
> (Ibid.)

To consider others as equals would have to mean that we are able to see them as just that, as simply others, without imprinting on them a connotation of value compared with the one we imprint on ourselves. But imprinting them with such a connotation has so far proved to be the most recurrent procedure. And this is explained by the fact that, apparently, not doing so leads us not to know how to compare, because it leads us to tolerate in others what for us are alien identity traits, sometimes so alien, says Castoriadis, that we consider them an "abomination".

In this way, we have almost always established others as inferior. This, Castoriadis adds, is not an inevitability but simply what has been most recurrent in human societies and their institutions.

The inferiority of others is but the other side of the affirmation of the self-truth of the institutions of Ego-society (in the sense in which Ego is spoken of in kinship systems) [...] a self-truth which is taken to exclude all others, which makes everything else a mistake [...] positive [...] [The] only foundation [of the social institution] is the belief in it and, more specifically, the fact that it claims to give meaning and make the world and life coherent makes it mortally endangered from the moment it is presented with the proof that there are other ways of making life and the world coherent and meaningful.

(Castoriadis, 2001: 22)

Regardless of whether or not this other shows us, from the outset or after the first contacts, that he or she has more numerical power, more weapons, more technical capacity than us, and regardless of whether he or she is aggressive towards us or not, we find his or her otherness so threatening that we take it as false, incorrect, inferior, inadmissible and intolerable.

In other words, the fact that one ethnic group or people has greater power than another and exercises it against the latter is not a *sine qua non* condition for there to be: (a) at the very core of the former and with regard to the latter, feelings and ideas that include the components of fear, rejection, inferiority, hatred or even a desire for extermination; and (b) at the very core of the latter and with respect to the former, almost the same feelings and ideas. The mere encounter between two culturally diverse peoples can perfectly well produce this imaginary of one towards the other, without the power or hegemony factor necessarily coming into play. This does not invalidate the fact that, in situations where the factors of power and subjugation come into play, the dominant people have a much greater capacity than the dominated to translate this rejectionist imaginary into mistreatment and discrimination, which can reach alarming levels of violence and cruelty.[2]

In short, the fear that the encounter with biological, mythical and cultural otherness implies for the habitat and for the collective identity of any people has been the most recurrent trigger, throughout human history, of the construction of the other as inferior.

It is this fear that leads us to construct, towards the other, multiple and diverse forms of exclusion, defined by Castoriadis as "the systematic denial, throughout history, of the idea – and of the practices associated with it – that the other is simply that: other" (Castoriadis, 2001: 19). Such forms of exclusion are always accompanied by a symbolic apparatus that creates prejudices and institutionalised phenomena of discrimination,[3] of which racism is one of the most recurrent, widespread and dangerous.

Prejudice

Prejudice is an attitude, judgement or feeling about a person that stems from a generalisation of attitudes or beliefs held about the group to which that person belongs. It involves the assumption that all members of that group are similar in a specific way.

In order to understand the roots and specificities of prejudice, it is first of all indispensable to situate it historically. Prejudicial expressions emerged either from intercultural encounters or from social conflicts based on them, which led them to exist and develop into what they are today. In many of these conflicts, the purpose of preserving the domination and hegemony of some groups over others led to the creation and spread of prejudice. This is why prejudices often attack those at the bottom of the socio-economic and socio-cultural ladder, but sometimes attack people belonging to scapegoated groups within the framework of diverse social, economic, political and cultural situations, and for reasons that are not necessarily those of class domination. This is the case, for example, with anti-Semitic prejudice.

Prejudices narrow our understanding of others as they bias our judgement of them. They predetermine why we do not want to approach them and also what we will discover about them when we approach and observe them.

This way of thinking promotes ignorance, degrades knowledge, excludes rather than includes, strains relationships and fosters rejection among human beings.

Gordon Allport, author of the now classic book *The Nature of Prejudice* (1954/1979), a pioneer on these issues, defined prejudice, in particular ethnic prejudice, as "an antipathy based on a faulty and inflexible generalisation. It may be felt or expressed. It may be directed at a group as a whole, or at an individual because he is a member of that group" (Allport, 1954/1979: 10).

From the point of view of social psychology, prejudice is defined by the analysis of the causes of a view of a person being constructed on the basis of elements that do not justify a legitimate judgement. Moreover, the generalisations on which prejudice is based are not only false but also inflexible.

This inflexibility is clearly illustrated in the example given in Allport's aforementioned book (1954/1979: 13):

MR X: The problem with Jews is that they only look after their own group.

MR Y: But the record of the *Community Chest* campaign shows that, proportionate to the size of their group, they give more generously to our community, in terms of charity, than non-Jews.

MR X: That proves that they are always trying to buy favours and meddle in Christian affairs. They think of nothing but money; that is why there are so many Jewish bankers.

MR Y: But a recent study shows that the percentage of Jews in the banking world is tiny, and smaller than the percentage of non-Jews.

MR X: That's precisely the point; they are not involved in respectable business; they are only in the film business or running *night clubs*.

As this example makes very clear, Mr X constructs very broad prejudices or judgements about Jews in order to justify his pejorative belief towards them. When Mr Y confronts him with verifiable facts, Mr X does not alter his prejudice, but simply moves the conversation towards one more negative aspect of the group they are talking about, so that this aspect again justifies his negative attitude towards Jews.

There is an important element in Allport's view of prejudice as a basically negative attitude, which is undoubtedly an elementary and primary response to the intrinsic fear that the other generates in us and the consequent uncertainty and insecurity that this fear provokes in us. This attitude causes people to resist the unknown, to resist change, to resist things and people that are different. It is a problem because it involves not understanding or wanting to understand the other, thinking and feeling that he or she is something he or she is not, and reacting to those ideas and feelings in ways that increase antagonism and conflict. It involves partiality and detachment. It leads us to reject the very possibility of placing ourselves in another's place and trying to understand who he or she is, what is wrong with him or her, and what he or she feels and thinks.

Its very existence places the object of prejudice at an unfair disadvantage in two possible ways:

a   Victims enter a space of non-civilisation or inhumanity that demeans their quality as people, as a result of the mere explicit prejudice created about them in the minds and feelings of many people who are different from them.
b   Victims may suffer negative and discriminatory treatment, based not on their own behaviour or circumstances but on the mere prejudice against them that is generalised, even to the point of denying them equal opportunities.

Often, prejudiced attitudes and feelings that are made explicit can turn into hate speech. It is true that, when people affected by hate speech have tried to convince the legislative system that it is necessary to legislate against this verbal or written phenomenon, or when they have filed a complaint before the judicial courts for the same reason, in general these two institutional instances of the state are not sympathetic to this cause. They argue that "it is mere discourse, without consequences in social practice", and that punishing it – if it has not affected any person in the exercise of their rights – does nothing more than attack freedom of expression, a human right considered fundamental within the framework of liberal-democratic legal-political systems. The questions that remain open here are: what should be the limits to freedom of expression in a democracy? And when can prejudice, despite being *only* a discursive manifestation, become so serious that it affects the right to non-discrimination of individuals?

There is a basic belief that the analysis of attitudes can predict behaviour, although the relationship between attitudes and behaviour is far more complex than this simple idea suggests (Jones, 1996: 143–150). However, there are some very clear behavioural manifestations of prejudice that lead to discrimination, understood as those actions that result in the characteristics and privileged position of one's own group being maintained at the expense of members of the group with which one compares oneself. And, as we know, discrimination is actionable in legal terms, whereas prejudice, per se, is not.

Stereotypes and Social Stereotyping

The tendency to assign traits, either positive or negative, to an entire group of people is one aspect of what is known as stereotyping. This is important in this topic as stereotypes are considered to be the locomotives of prejudice.

The original definition of stereotype is a metal plate that is used to duplicate pages. "Stereotyping" or the action of stereotyping is

> the procedure used in the printing industry to reproduce a typesetting. This consists of pressing, against the type, a special cardboard or a sheet of other material, which serves as a mould to empty the molten metal and to be able to reproduce one and multiple times, on the basis of this technique, each printed page.
>
> (*Dictionary of the Royal Academy of the Spanish Language*, www.rae.es/desen/estereotipo)

When we stamp every member of a group as a duplicate of every other member of the same group, we are social stereotyping, creating a human stereotype. On this basis, we do not see each member of a group other than our own as she or he really is. What we see is the image of him or her as it appears filtered in our minds and feelings by this mental picture of the group we have stereotyped.

> Stereotypes establish identifications between people who most likely have nothing to do with each other, but they also frame an expectation that may well not correspond to the people they refer to. What do we know about a person when we know that he or she is African American, female, gay, lesbian, Hindu, Jewish or poor? We know nothing, but we can suspect some things about him or her. We may suspect that the Jew is concerned about money or is intelligent. We can believe that the gay man has artistic qualities or is shy or morally perverse. We may imagine the woman to be emotional, conformist and nurturing. We may assume that the African American is athletic, musically talented, aggressive, unintelligent, etc.
>
> These assumptions, or to put it more neutrally, these *expectations*, shape what we perceive, subsequently influencing our judgement and our behaviour towards a person.
>
> (Jones, 1996: 165)

Social psychologists Lee, Jussim and McCauley (1995) catalogue the reasons why stereotypes are a real social problem: (a) they are factually incorrect. It cannot be true that everyone in a group possesses specific traits. Not even one of the most characteristic phenotypic traits of a given human group – the darkest skin, the slanted eyes, the straightest hair – is possessed by absolutely all its members; (b) they are illogical in origin, because they emanate not from personal experience but from hearsay or second-hand information; (c) they are based on prejudice and, in this sense, only reinforce previously established beliefs; (d) they encourage their bearers to be irrationally resistant to new information that contradicts stereotypes; (e) they exaggerate the differences between groups; (f) they are ethnocentric; (g) they are generally based on a biologistic essentialism, as they assume that the origins of differences between groups are, in the first instance, genetic and, therefore, immutable and, consequently, irreconcilable; and, finally, (h) they underestimate the variability that exists in Others. They have the idea that all members of other groups "look identical" or "are identical"; they encourage self-fulfilling prophecies.

In other words, if we use stereotypes to guide our expectations or our suspicions, we are prone to see what we expect to see before we confront the stereotypes with the facts.[4]

Although stereotyping has such negative consequences in the world, it is done all the time and everywhere. It seems that our fearful and prejudiced way of looking at and valuing otherness leads to a tendency to simplify the complexity and heterogeneity of all that part of the human social world that does not directly concern us. We thus exaggerate the homogeneity of people. We proceed to a kind of "cognitive greed" (Fiske and Taylor, 1991: 139) that leads us to rely more on stereotypes than on what would be the result of a real and as objective as possible effort to analyse and judge each event, object, idea or person in itself.

In this way, we establish in our minds and feelings an order in the external world. And although this order exists only in this dimension of our life, it does not necessarily lead us to change this practice, nor does it allow us to even glimpse the possibility that we are making a mistake. On the contrary, what seems to matter more to us is to confirm the correctness of our prejudices, on which we confer the status of an accurate reflection of reality, of the truth about it.

Although there are different theoretical and disciplinary approaches to study and understand stereotypes – for example, the cognitive (Hamilton and Trolier, 1986: 133)[5] or *the psychodynamic*[6] – it is to the socio-cultural perspective that this work is preferably ascribed. The national, ethnic and socio-cultural milieu in which each individual develops provides a background context the values and beliefs of which are undoubtedly determinant of the way in which, from childhood onwards, he or she develops specific collective views and beliefs about other communities.

From this perspective, a stereotype is seen as emanating from the socio-cultural context in which we live. Stereotypes help us define the norms of our own groups, in part by distinguishing those characteristics of others that differentiate them from us. The perceptions that one group has of another or of the individuals in it reflect communal patterns of beliefs that, therefore, establish *consensual stereotypes* (Gardner, 1994). These, in our society, play an important role as a result of both intra-group and inter-group socialisation patterns and the effects of media portrayals of different groups.

In short, stereotypes play a fundamental role in our daily lives. It has been shown to what extent they affect the type of information we integrate and remember and the type of information we do not integrate and do not remember, but also how they influence how we interpret this or that type of information and how we use it to make judgements. As stereotypes can and often do operate at the level of the unconscious and, from there, influence our thinking, our feelings and our behaviours, we are often unaware that what is happening is that we are looking at others through the lens of stereotypical prejudice.

In all these ways, "stereotypes are some of the crucial elements that allow us to understand the perennial power of prejudice" (Jones, 1996: 202).

"Race" and Racism in Relation to Ethnicity, Class and Power

It is difficult to know when, in ancient human history, human groups began to be distinct in terms of, among other things, their phenotypic characteristics, such as skin colour, hair type, facial features and so on. It is evident that, at the beginning of human time, the phenotypic characteristics of those who formed our species, all born on the African continent, must not have been very different. They began to vary more and more as time went on, as different groups of humans dispersed across the five continents, as each group had been living for many generations (60,000 years or so) in different natural habitats, with different climates and altitudes, and eating different fruits and animals. All this led the human bodies, subjected to different environmental conditions, to adapt to them in the best possible evolutionary way. Thus, skin colours, nose and mouth shapes, muscle structures and hair types became different (Mayr, 2001; King, 2007).

When this happened in a sufficiently noticeable way, at moments of encounter between different human groups, each of them was confronted not only with the cultural and identity difference of the other but also with their phenotypic difference.

There is a debate among scholars as to when these phenotypic variations began to play a vital role in establishing the way some groups regarded others as inferior during intercultural encounters. Some (Wieviorka, 1994) believe that this did not begin to occur until the full birth of the modern era – that is, with the political and social ideas and practices associated with the Enlightenment. It was hand in hand with these ideas and practices that the concept of race was born, in the sense that, socially speaking, it remains to this day: a set of people who share the same biological, genetic characteristics, which are natural, innate and, therefore, immovable, and which are manifested at a glance in skin colour and phenotypic traits. This is a concept loaded with the idea that, although human beings, within the framework of a nation-state, are all equal before the law, this equality can neither be conceived nor applied legally and politically between those who belong to different "races", as they are marked by a natural essence of inferiority or superiority.

Others (Wade, 1997: 14–15) consider that this phenomenon – which properly marks the birth of racism – occurred at the time of Europe's colonial encounters with the New World:

> Races, racial categories and racial ideologies are those that elaborate social constructions, drawing on the particular aspects of phenotypic variation that were transformed into vital signifiers of difference during European colonial encounters with the new world.

Still others take a similar position to Castoriadis's:

> The only true specificity of racism (in relation to the different varieties of hatred of others), the only decisive one, as the logicians say, is this: true racism does not allow others to abjure (or they are persecuted or suspected when they have already abjured: the converts). [...] We would find racism less abominable if it were content to have forced conversions (like Christianity, Islam, etc.). However, racism does not desire the conversion of others, what it desires is their death [...] for racism, the other is unconvertible. It is immediately apparent the quasi necessity of underpinning the racist imaginary on constant (and therefore irreversible) physical characteristics.
>
> (Castoriadis, 2001: 24–25)

Castoriadis thus states that, although not all phenomena of hatred or exclusion between culturally diverse peoples or beings can be classified as racist, neither can it in any way be said that racism is peculiar only to modernity, as there are multiple phenomena in pre-modern history that show the kind of hatred he is referring to here.

In my view, racism is a way of thinking, feeling and acting that is based on a specific characteristic of human difference that has been called "racial". Since the mid 18th century, the division of humanity into "races" has been one of the most effective means of establishing hierarchies between human groups, falsely positing that there are inferior and superior "races". This way of classifying humanity has strongly contributed to the creation of many inequalities and injustices, as the idea has been internalised that some people are worth less because of a biological characteristic anchored in their "nature".

Racist thinking places people's bodies in a defined place according to their appearance, as it maintains that people's physical or biological characteristics are directly associated with their practices, their ways of behaving and even their intelligence. This way of thinking and acting implies rejection, hierarchisation, domination and inferiorisation of some towards others, for supposedly biological reasons, establishing relations of power and domination that are manifested in practices and behaviours considered normal. This deepens inequalities and justifies them, as it seems that some have the right to better living conditions than others. In everyday life, we can see how racism is exercised (thought, felt and acted) by specific people against specific individuals or communities. However, racism is not only present in the particular acts of some people whom we can identify as racists.

> Racism is structural in scope, i.e. it goes beyond individual actions. To say that racism is a structural system means that this model of understanding human difference has ordered society, has filtered into the construction of social institutions (such as the family or the school) and political institutions (such as the state and its governing bodies) and has become naturalised in ideas, feelings and everyday practices. As a result, this system benefits certain populations that it considers racially superior, to the detriment of populations that it regards as inferior because of their supposed "race", having as an effect the continuous reproduction of hierarchies and inequalities between racialised populations and individuals.
>
> (Gall, Iturriaga, Morales and Rodríguez, 2021: 8–9)

Today, we know that the concept of "race", constructed as we have described it here, has no meaning in terms of contemporary science, as biology and genetics have clearly shown how genetic variations are greater within a human group that we have tended to call "race" – blacks, whites, yellows and reds – than between one of these groups and others.

However, despite this, the notion of race continues to have an important socio-cultural significance. We continue to make racial affirmations, accompanied by their essentialist implications. "Race" is, therefore, a cultural construct, an idea. And, like many other ideas, the idea of race turns out to carry enormous weight in reality, because those who believe in it behave as if races really exist.

If we continue to see society as racialised, it is because there is a socio-historical legacy of the concept of race that, today, three centuries into the modern era and in the midst of globalisation, is already embedded in the cultural ethos of the world, because evidence suggests that people still tend to think of human beings as divided into separate types by essences, whether biologically, psychologically or culturally determined; and, finally, because the meaning and utility of the concept and the idea of race have been perpetuated over time through processes that are generated and reproduced through institutional practices and social policies that implicitly and explicitly recognise race and use it to achieve social, political and economic goals.[7]

Teun Van Dijk (1987), a specialist, among other things, in the analysis of racialised and racist discourse, suggests that racial prejudice, diffused through discourse and operating at an individual level through interpersonal and inter-group dynamics, is one of the central mechanisms that sustain racialised societies. The language, images and stories present in formal and informal conversations and in government and media discourse reinforce racial differences between groups and associate specific cultural traits and differential values with each group.

However, race, ethnicity, class and culture are intertwined in ways that make it difficult to isolate causal influences and identify the best ways to change racialisation in our societies.

It has not been easy to distinguish the concept of race from that of "ethnicity", two concepts that illustrate diverse but closely intertwined social realities. As Peter Wade says, the term ethnicity is a concept that has often been used in place of race. But where, if anywhere, does the specificity of ethnicity reside? What kind of social construct is ethnicity? Where does cultural difference reside? Cultural difference extends across geographical space, Wade answers. People use their location, or rather their supposed origin, to talk about difference and equality. The quintessential ethnic question is: where are you from?

However, according to Banks, ethnicity

> is a collection of statements [...] about boundaries, otherness, goals and achievements, self and identity, descent and classification, which has been constructed both by the ethnic subject and by outsiders: anthropologists, "others" and the media.
>
> (1996)

Race and ethnicity are thus distinct concepts. They are both social constructs, but different social constructs. I agree with Wade that race is a social construct based on ideas about innate, biological, natural difference. Ethnicity, on the other hand, is a social construct based on a specific notion of cultural differentiation, built on the notion of "place of origin", in which social relations respond first and foremost to spatially determined geographical differences.

In other words, the ethnicity of a group is generally contrasted with the group's "racial status" on the basis of biological versus cultural considerations. So-called "racial identity" is often seen as anchored in what are defined as racially determined adaptations to the socio-political and cultural constructs of a society. Ethnic identity is often viewed in a similar way, but is more generally expressed in terms of those dynamic forces that define people on the basis of their ethnic group (Casas and Pyltuk, 1995: 159).[8]

Although distinct, these concepts and the realities they express are often closely related. It is clear that racial and ethnic identifications overlap in both theory and practice. To replace these terms with one another is to deny the specific role played in history by racial identifications or by the various types of discrimination based on them. "This does not mean that ethnic histories cannot be long and conflictive, but I think it is necessary to highlight the history of race by calling it by its name" (Wade, 1997: 6).

We often try to use the concept "ethnicity" instead of that of "race" because race has very negative connotations and is associated with limitations imposed by genetic immutability. But such conceptual juggling does not get us very far and tends to negate an important part of international and interethnic conflicts, as the meaning that the social construct "race" continues to have in real life is considerable, despite its flawed conceptual basis and negative history. Since the beginning of the modern liberal era, at the individual level, people believe that other socio-cultural groups are inferior and that their own is superior, precisely by virtue of "race". At the institutional level, racialised thinking and practices, whether intentional or unintentional, confer privilege and advantage to one racial group – which is sometimes also ethnic – over others. At the cultural level, the dominant culture's values, symbols, traditions and world-view reinforce the notion of racial superiority/inferiority and disseminate these ideas through culture.

On the other hand, it has been easy to disentangle what has been called "race" from class, given that the history of racism has shown how, in many parts of the world, racial-ethnic minorities are generally located in the lower economic strata. The question is, which came first: race or class? How much of what is seen as racial inequities can be attributed to the cumulative effects of a long-standing racialised culture that has resulted in placing the peoples who are victims of racist discrimination on the lowest rungs of the social and economic ladder? Or, how much of what we see today as racial inequalities linked to class inequalities can be seen as originating in the class logic underlying the development of an economic and socio-cultural system that has made racism a central tool of the exploitation of the labour of others?

Classical Marxist theory argues that racial categories were created either by the European colonisers in order to better dominate and over-exploit a part of humanity (Quijano, 2000), or by the bourgeoisie, in order to better dominate a specific part of the labour force and to deepen the premodern colonial enterprise, conquering new markets and subjecting the aborigines of those colonised lands to a regime of imperialist exploitation. Today, we know that, even if this view is not totally incorrect, it oversimplifies historical reality for several reasons: because ideological categories can affect economic factors in the same way as the latter can affect the former, and because racial identifications can be different either during different periods within the colonial or capitalist phase of the history of a region that has become a nation-state, or in some of the regions of a country during the same period of its capitalist development.

In my view, class logic and cultural logic mutually determine, complement and constantly feed back into each other in determining institutionally framed racialised and class practices, and the attitudes and beliefs about race that individuals adopt. The racialised form that colonisation took could not have been as it was if there had not been a broad racialised cultural context that shaped the perceptions, feelings and ideas of the colonisers towards the colonised, colouring them with racism. Moreover, given that the economic and political logic of colonisation was that of the expansion of monarchical power that entailed the over-exploitation of the human and material resources of the colonised territories, the racialised cultural logic found extremely fertile ground to develop.

Racial identity describes a set of racially determined adaptations to socio-political and cultural constructions of race in our society (Helms, 1995). All groups that can be described by racial labels or as socio-racial groups can be characterised by their racialised adaptations and forms of socialisation. To put it in plain terms, who someone is depends, in part, on what racial group he or she belongs to, what socio-political and economic position that group has in society, and how people socialise within that group and in relation to other groups.

After these necessary digressions, we come to racism. Racism is extremely complex and multifaceted, and it is also multidimensional, so to speak of "racisms" is a better representation of the reality of the phenomenon.

To put it in the words of Pierre André Taguieff, author of the book *La force du préjugé. Essai sur le racisme et ses doubles* (1988),

> we will distinguish, for example, *classical*, biological and inequitable *racism* from *neo-racism*, differentialist and cultural, which does not biologise what is different, or differentialist racism based on *a denial of humanity*. Let us clarify this fundamental distinction: racism derived from abstract universalism does not recognise *the specific dignity* of this or that group, and is identified by its absolute rejection of the right to difference, by its denial of human diversity as a value (it is therefore *heterophobic*); whereas racism derived from the radical differentialist vision, which consists in sacralising phenotypical, cultural differences between human groups, does not recognise the equal *human dignity* of the members of all groups, and thus denies the common nature of human beings (it could be considered *heterophile*). We should also be careful not to confuse *exploitative racism* (illustrated by European colonialism or modern slavery systems) and exterminatory racism, which includes a more or less explicit genocidal project (the Nazi regime is its most visible historical illustration).
>
> (2001: 4)

In any case, for all their differences, racism is the most basic and destructive form that prejudice takes. While prejudiced thinking and feelings can extend to any dimension in which people evaluate and judge other people, and even things and events around them, racist prejudice goes much further than that. It goes beyond demeaning others by dehumanising and demonising those who are judged as "different".

When the nation-state affirms its national identity on the basis of "pure blood", the so-called "racial Other" becomes the feared enemy. Because prejudice thrives on process, it seeks simple grounds for discriminating between the I/Us and the Other(s). And, once such racism is embedded in a society, it is difficult, even for those "judicious" – more objective – people within it, "not to accept in some way 'the ground of truth' or the assumption behind the stereotype" (Jones, 1996: xviii). We create racial – not just ethnic – categories, and the people who belong to them are given racial-ethnic labels – a process known as *racial profiling*, which in some countries, such as Mexico, should be more properly called *racial-ethnic-class profiling*.

Racist practice is built on a cultural context armed with racial prejudice. But, while racism resembles prejudice in certain respects, it has a broader and more complex meaning,[9] for what transforms racial prejudice into racism is the imposition of some groups' power and hegemony over others.[10] And, when these are organised around racialised categories, then the values held by racist thinking become structural factors in the society in question.

Conclusions

Prejudice is an almost inevitable consequence of being human and living in a society made up of diverse peoples. Social and institutional structures and patterns feed perceptions and social processes in ways that fuel prejudice. The implicit action of stereotyping has been shown to occur in important ways in relation to the perceptions and judgements that dominant ethnic-racial groups have about members of ethnic and racial minority groups. It can also occur among minority ethnic and racial groups. These processes occur at the most elementary levels of thinking and cognitive judgement but reflect cultural and identity patterns that are subtly but consistently represented in political-institutional arrangements and social processes.

Racism and racial prejudice work together. At the macro level of society, culture shapes institutional arrangements and imbues them with racialised meanings and essences. At the micro level, individuals are imbued with this racialised milieu and behave towards ethnically and racially different others in ways that have been previously influenced by the way this milieu has conditioned them. In this way, the role of race in culture and institutions is constantly evolving and changing, redefining itself once again in each generation. While the basic equations of race are modified and transformed, they are not destroyed.

To say the same thing, but now in Taguieff's words, "despite half a century of unanimous condemnation, racism has not disappeared. It has metamorphosed, to the point of sometimes being unrecognisable [...] It has become a conceptually vague term, which gives the impression of being part of the landscape" (2001).

However, simultaneously with this phenomenon, after the Nazi Holocaust and many of the racist phenomena of recent years (the Balkan war, Rwanda, the Guatemalan genocide etc.), an anti-racist consciousness has been created, has grown and has been internalised by numerous groups and organisations and by the legislations of many democratic-pluralist countries. One part of the action of anti-racists has been to refute, on the basis of current scientific knowledge, all the false theses that structure the various racisms, showing them for what they are: myths, prejudices and stereotypes. A second part of this action consists of a series of theoretical, political, cultural, legal and organisational proposals that many groups have been putting forward.

The definition of the tasks and aims of anti-racism – I continue along the path opened by Taguieff – must be rethought, in principle, in relation to the answers given to the following fundamental questions: to what extent is racism the product of a cognitive tendency peculiar to the human species, to what extent is it a constant in human thought and the human construction of identity-otherness? To what extent is it a phenomenon specific to different cultures and different historical periods? To what extent is it a phenomenon specific to a historical period, linked to the development of modernity and its need to find ways of not including those who, in pre-modern times, it had learned to despise, hate or over-exploit?

This reflection should be followed by another, accompanied by anti-racist actions applied to each case in relation to the varied racist representations that are produced in diverse social, political and cultural contexts and show the multidimensional nature of racism: attitudes and feelings; behaviours, conducts or practices; ideological discourses; the legal-political modality of the nation-state and institutional functioning.

As Michel Ignatieff wrote:

> the needs of human beings are contradictory, specifically [...] the need for freedom and the need for belonging or rootedness are theoretically irreconcilable [...] politics is [...] the perpetually recommenced attempt, in practice, to reconcile what is theoretically irreconcilable, namely the incompatibility of the human needs for freedom and security, for individuation and belonging.
>
> (Ignatieff, 1986: 9–10)

In today's world, this contradiction is clearly reflected in the world of racism and anti-racism. Each of the major human forms of belonging and defence of identity has its own universe of values and its own ideology. On the one hand, the defence of identities based on blood and/or culture in the traditional-communitarian universe – the space of which is often that of the nation-state – is corrupted into the racism of exclusion and/or extermination. On the other hand, the defence of reason, ordered in the sense of an individual-centred, so-called universalist universe, ends up defending European provincialism as if it were planetary, and is corrupted into racism of assimilation and the unequal legitimisation of imperialism.

However, reconciling these two polarised forms of human solidarity, tribal and global, is an urgent task. A necessary first step is to prevent both fronts from giving in to "racist temptations". One is to cling to the tribal idea (Maalouf, 1999) that an ethnicity or people should continue to operate as a consanguineous family; another is to disavow any group smaller than the human species, as if there were nothing important between the individual and the human race, which in fact hides the fabrication of one group – complex and multifaceted, but ultimately Western – as the normative model and ideal of humanity.

> For this, it is necessary to distinguish authentic universalism from its instrumentalisation at the hands of Western ethnocentrism, which means admitting the legitimate critique of the simulacra of the universal and not confusing it with the nihilistic rejection of any demand for universality. To reject outright an authentic universalism would be as much as to resign oneself to the fact that individual and collective forces would confront each other to infinity in a space of pure violence in which all communication would be, as a matter of principle, excluded.
>
> (Taguieff, 1988: 481)

But it is also essential to stop ruling the world on the basis of the nationalist principle, which also represents pure violence, because it does not give any place to the claims of ethnic and cultural minorities.

We should be able to build mediating communities of universalism, in which community integration appears as a necessary condition for a horizon of universality – that is to say, where the community of belonging exists and is respected in its identity, but where it does not have itself as a finality, where the finality is its transactional character with the world-community.

In order to think of a cultural democracy, we need to de-absolutise, de-essentialise the principle of difference, which would thus be integrated, but as a relativising factor, in a non-ethnocentric humanism.

This requires not overemphasising the role of diversity and differentiation, but not failing to recognise the reality of differences; differences that, in order to have a transactional value towards a planetary humanism, must be compensatory to each other. As Boaventura de Sousa Santos would say, each culture must modestly recognise both its own successes and its own limitations, and that it needs, therefore, to compensate for the deficiencies of other cultural voices, as well as to be compensated by them (1998: 183).

In terms of its approach to human affairs, the universalism we must seek must be neither essentialist nor ethnocentric; it should demand and defend the transcendental communicative capacity and exercise of all, both individuals and groups, a communicative exercise that in no way excludes respect for differences, but, on the contrary, requires it.

But this universalism must be more than humanistic; it must go beyond anthropocentrism. Science is discovering day by day that the social organisation of other animals, insects and bacteria that share this planet Earth with our species allows us to better understand human societies (Wilson, 2012: 10), but also, and above all, we must not forget what Carl Sagan masterfully reminded us in his speech *The Pale Blue Dot* (1994): All of human history and existence is contained "in a speck of dust suspended in a ray of sunlight", and "there is perhaps no better demonstration of the folly of human assumptions than this distant image of our small world":

> Earth is a very small stage in a vast cosmic arena. Think of the rivers of blood shed by all those generals and emperors, so that, in glory and triumph, they could become momentary masters of a fraction of a point. Think of the endless cruelties visited by the inhabitants of one corner of that pixel upon the barely distinguishable inhabitants of some other corner; how frequent their misunderstandings, how greedily they have killed one another, how fervent their hatred.
>
> Our posturing, our imagined self-importance, the illusion that we have a privileged position in the Universe, is challenged by this point of pale light. Our planet is a solitary speck in the great enveloping cosmic darkness.
>
> [...]
>
> Whether we like it or not, for the moment Earth is where we have to stay.
>
> It has been said that astronomy is a humbling and character-building experience. Perhaps there is no better demonstration of the foolishness of human prejudice than this distant image of our tiny world. To me, it underlines our responsibility to treat each other kindlier, and to succeed in preserving and appreciating the pale blue dot, the only home we have ever known.[11]

Notes

1 There are some exceptions to this rule, such as the perception that many already colonised peoples have of those who have conquered and subjugated them as superior to them. See Fanon (2009).

2 "Human societies are generally characterised, irrespective of their differences in many areas, by the following three attributes: there exist within them hierarchies based on group solidarities in which at least one group dominates all others and in which that group enjoys a privileged position in terms of [material, political and cultural] goods. [...] In this hierarchical system, it also happens that at least one group is in a subordinate position and enjoys a negatively disproportionate share of [material, political and cultural] goods; different groups compete for scarce symbolic and material resources, seeking to improve their respective positions within society relative to valued goods and, finally, as part of this competitive relationship, groups use ideological strategies; concepts of national, racial or ethnic superiority or specific political ideologies, which result in opposing policies that are implemented by the groups with which the group itself competes and which advance the privileged position of these groups.

"The group in power will seek to control both materially and symbolically those social instruments that serve to maintain its group domination, and will develop policies, beliefs and myths that legitimise and perpetuate its domination. These policies or beliefs are promulgated by those at the top of the hierarchy who define a general theory of society. All members of society and all other groups are subject to them and therefore tend to believe in them or support them, in varying ways and to varying degrees. And even groups at the bottom of the hierarchy may come to support policies that perpetuate their oppressed status" (Sidanius, 1993).

3 It should be noted that, according to the *Dictionary of the Royal Academy of the Spanish Language*, the word "discriminate" does not necessarily have, etymologically, a pejorative connotation, as it is synonymous with "differentiate" and "distinguish". These two verbs illustrate the act of registering that one thing, person or situation is just that, distinct, other, different from the first. However, the reason why we have culturally constructed the verb "discriminate" with a pejorative connotation is precisely because, as Castoriadis puts it, we are apparently incapable of comparing and differentiating without regarding the others as inferior or even hating them.

4 This can go even further and have more serious consequences: by dint of being recurrently targeted by stereotypes, stereotypists may introject them, even if they are not saying who they really are. In doing so, they may behave in ways that confirm them, even when they are trying hard to contradict these expectations (Steele and Aronson, 1995).

5 This type of approach sees the stereotype simply as a cognitive representation of social information about people and human groups. As such, a stereotype is "a cognitive structure that contains the perceiver's knowledge, beliefs and expectations about another human group".

6 This type of approach sees the stereotype as a mechanism that serves the purposes of ego defence. In other words, it sees stereotypes as "protectors" of the ego against its perceived threats from others and as reinforcers of the self. It also sees them as instruments to derogate other stereotypes and thus to elevate the self or one's membership group.

7 One of the most useful definitions of this concept is "the social production of human groups in racial terms" (Campos, 2012). Racialisation is a very particular and specific way of viewing and labelling people's bodies in terms of "races". This means that human groups are conceived as if each of those who inhabit them belong to the same "race". Thus, when a person sees another person as belonging to a specific "race" and assigns stereotypes that fit this generalisation, he or she is racialising that person.

"Beyond an act of individual classification, racialisation is a social process through which countries and societies are structured, determining that within them there are certain racial divisions between their groups, and that these characterise them and largely explain the differences and inequalities that exist between them. Each country has a different model of racialisation that responds to its conformation, its history and its identity, and that begins at the end of the 18th and beginning of the 19th century" (Gall, Iturriaga, Morales, and Rodríguez, 2021: 48–49).

8 Casas and Pyltuk define ethnic identity as follows: "A set of ideas about the self that relate specifically to membership in an ethnic group [...] and that relate directly to one's knowledge of one's own membership in that group and the knowledge, understanding, values, behaviours and feelings of pride that are direct implications of that membership" (1995).

9 Van den Berghe defines racism as: "Any set of beliefs that genetically transmitted organic differences (whether real or imagined) between human groups are intrinsically associated with the presence or absence of some relevant social skills or

characteristics, making these differences a legitimate basis for individual distinctions between groups socially defined as races" (Van den Berghe, 1967: 101).

10 Ethnocentrism simply refers to the preference one has for one's own way of life or culture. However, the ethnocentrism of one group is a benign preference only when there is no contact between that group and other groups of people imbued with alternative ethnocentric inclinations. When groups are in contact, their differences stand out, and the simple preference, combined with issues of power and control, escalates into the construction of privilege for the *in-group*. When the privileged status of the *in-group* coincides with power and control in a given society, and when the facts of power and control are formalised as natural and right then groups adopt practices and values that serve to perpetuate domination and control (Sidanius, 1993). "The cumulative instruments and practices of a group's domination describe the principle of hegemony. And hegemonic domination is the way in which a group remains in power by whatever means possible. That is, if, at a given time and in a given situation, the old strategies of domination – slavery, overt racism, legal control, and oppression and intimidation – become less viable means of securing domination, new and more subtle ways of securing those strategies emerge" (Jones, 1996: 416).

11 See www.inspiredspeeches.com/education/carl-sagan-pale-blue-dot

References

Allport, Gordon, *The Nature of Prejudice*, Reading, MA: Addison-Wesley, 1954/1979.

Banks, Marcus, *Ethnicity: Anthropological Constructions*, London: Routledge, 1996.

Campos, A., Racialización, racialismo y racismo: un discernimiento necesario (Racialisation, racialism and racism: a necessary discernment), Universidad de la Habana, no. 273, 2012.

Casas, J.M. and Pyltuk, S.D., "Hispanic Identity Development: Implications for Research and Practice", in J.G. Ponterotto, J.M. Casas, L.A. Suzuki, and C.M. Alexander (Eds.), *Handbook of Multicultural Counseling*, pp. 155–180, Thousand Oaks, CA: Sage, 1995.

Castoriadis, Cornelius, "Reflexiones en torno al racismo" (Reflections on racism), in O. Gall (Coord.), *Racismo y mestizaje, Debate Feminista* (Racism and Miscegenation, Feminist Debate), October, pp. 15–29, Mexico City, 2001.

Clastres, Pierre, *La Société contre l'État* (Society versus the state), Paris: Minuit, 1974.

Fanon, Frantz, *Piel negra, máscaras blancas* (Black skin, white masks), Madrid: Ediciones Akal, 2009.

Fiske, S.T. and Taylor, S.E., *Social Cognition*, New York: McGraw-Hill, 1991.

Fossaert, Robert, *Les Structures idéologiques* (Ideological structures), Paris: Les Éditions du Seuil, 1983.

Gall, O., Iturriaga, E., Morales, D. and Rodríguez, J., What is Racism and How Does it Manifest Itself?Mexico: CONAPRED, 2021. www.conapred.org.mx/documentos_cedoc/Queycomo_manifiesta_racismo_02_WEB.Ax.pdf

Gardner, R.C., "Stereotypes as Consensual Beliefs", in M.P. Zanna and J.M. Olson (Eds.), *The Psychology of Prejudice. The Ontario Symposium*, Vol. 7, pp. 1–27, Hillside, NJ: Erlbaum Associates, 1994.

Hamilton, D.L. and Trolier, T.K., "Stereotypes and Stereotyping: An Overview of the Cognitive Approach", in J.F. Dovidio and S.L. Gaertner (Eds.), *Prejudice, Discrimination and Racism*, pp. 127–163, Orlando, FL: Academic Press, 1986.

Hardwick, Charles S., *Semiotics and Significs: Correspondence between Charles S. Pierce and Lady Victoria Welby*, Bloomington: Indiana University Press, 1977.

Helms, J.E., "An Update of Helms' White and People of Color Racial Identity Models", in J.G. Ponterotto, J.M. Casas, L.A. Suzuki and C.M. Alexander (Eds.), *Handbook of Multicultural Counseling*, pp. 155–180, Thousand Oaks, CA: Sage, 1995.

Ignatieff, Michel, *La Liberté d'être humain. Essai sur le désir et le besoin* (The Freedom to be Human: An Essay on Desire and Need), Paris: La Découverte, 1986.

Jones, James, *Prejudice and Racism*, New York: McGraw-Hill, 1996.

King, Russell (Ed.), *Atlas of Human Migration*, Ontario: Firefly Books, 2007.

Kroeber, A.L. and Kluckhohn, C., *Culture: A Critical Review of Concepts and Definitions*, New York: Random House, 1952.

Lacan, Jacques, "Le stade du miroir comme formateur de la fonction du je, telle qu'elle nous est révélée dans l'expérience psychanalytique" (The mirror stage as formative of the function of the I, as it is revealed to us in psychoanalytic experience), in *Écrits*, Paris: Seuil, 1966.

Lee, Y., Jussim, L.J. and McCauley, C.R. (Eds.), *Stereotype Accuracy: Toward Appreciating Group Differences*, Washington, DC: American Psychological Association, 1995.

Maalouf, Amin, *Identidades Asesinas* (Killer identities), Madrid: Alianza Editorial, 1999.

Mayr, Ernst, *What Evolution Is*, New York: Basic Books, 2001.

Quijano, Aníbal, "Colonialidad del poder, eurocentrismo y América Latina" (Coloniality of power, Eurocentrism and Latin America), in Edgardo Lander (Ed.), *La colonialidad del saber: eurocentrismo y ciencias sociales. Perspectivas Latinoamericanas* (The coloniality of knowledge: Eurocentrism and the social sciences. Latin American Perspectives), Buenos Aires: CLASCO, Consejo Latinoamericano de Ciencias Sociales, 2000.

Sagan, Carl, *Pale Blue Dot: A Vision of the Human Future in Space*, New York: Ballantine Books, 1994.

Sidanius, J., "The Psychology of Group Conflict and the Dynamics of Oppression: A Social Dominance Perspective", in S. Iynengar and W. J. McGuire (Eds.), *Explorations in Political Psychology*, pp. 183–219, Durham, NC: Duke University Press, 1993.

Santos, Boaventura de Sousa, *La Globalización del Derecho. Los nuevos caminos de la regulación y la emancipación* (The globalisation of law. The new paths of regulation and emancipation), Colombia: ILSA, 1998.

Steele, C. M. and Aronson, J., "Stereotype Threat and the Intellectual Test Performance of African Americans", *Journal of Personality and Social Psychology*, 1, pp. 281–289, 1995.

Taguieff, Pierre André, *La force du préjugé, essai sur le racisme et ses doubles* (The power of prejudice, an essay on racism and its doubles), Paris: La Découverte, 1988.

Taguieff, Pierre André, "El racismo" (Racism), in O. Gall (Coord.), *Racismo y mestizaje, Debate Feminista* (Racism and miscegenation, feminist debate), October, pp. 3–14, Mexico City, 2001.

Van Den Berghe, Pierre, *Race and Racism. A Comparative Perspective*, New York: Wiley, 1967.

Van Dijk, Teun, *Communicating Racism: Ethnic Prejudice in Thought and Talk*, Newbury Park, CA: Sage, 1987.

Wade, Peter, *Race and Ethnicity in Latin America*, Chicago, IL: Pluto Press, 1997.

Wieviorka, Michel, "Qué es el racismo" (What is racism?), in A. Castellanos Guerrero (Coord.), *Estudios Sociológicos* (Sociological studies), Vol. XII, No 34, January–April, México: El Colegio de México, 1994.

Wilson, Edward Osborne, *The Social Conquest of the Earth*, W.W. Norton, 2012.

Chapter 3

Prejudice as a Basis for Discrimination

Fanny Blanck-Cereijido

The issue of prejudice and discrimination encompasses the individual psyche and the social imaginary, as each society is constituted of its values and its concepts of justice, logic, and aesthetics, so that it seems that the inferiority of the other is the reverse of the affirmation of one's own truth. It is a short distance from here to others being attributed an evil, perverse essence.[1]

Prejudice can have different meanings and requires different strategies for its understanding and management, according to the psychic space in which it operates: in individual subjects, in intersubjective relations or in the trans-subjective spaces that constitute us as social subjects.

The term prejudice implies the idea of a judgement that precedes one's own experience, which corresponds to the Kantian a priori; it captures the beliefs, values, and reference categories of the world of each subject, and depends on the words and concepts in which that subject is born and, thus, immersed. Prejudice provides an order and discrimination of the facts and factors that each person must evaluate for their understanding of the world around them, which is why it is indispensable for thought, as well as helping to protect self-definition and one's own limits. This classification prior to individual judgement places beliefs and convictions in a system of values accepted or rejected by the family and society that precede an individual. In this way, he or she is conditioned in his or her beliefs and values by family and social belonging, which in turn are the effect of conscious and unconscious transgenerational transmission.

The certainties provided by prejudices are uncritically incorporated beliefs, immovable traditions.[2] On the other hand, the judgement described by Freud as a judgement of attribution and existence, allows us to discriminate, to attribute values, to establish categories, and to distinguish an external object from a desired one, and it is modifiable by new knowledge or reasoning.

To assume that one's own view is the correct one and that the values of one's own community are real, objective, and natural values is a widespread way of looking at the world and is designated as an ethnocentric stance.[3] It is valid to discuss these questions because history is made by economic and social factors, but ideas are also decisive acts, events, and part of the driving force of historical fact.

DOI: 10.4324/9781003291978-4

When the one who assigns a negative value to a community or group with characteristics that are foreign to him or her possesses the force to exercise discrimination, contempt, and violence, we are faced with malignant prejudice. The wielder of prejudice and destructive force will attack and eliminate the object of hatred and contempt.

It is important to find the specific events or situations that link common prejudices, such as preferences, affinities, and customs, with malignant forms of violence and destruction.

In psychoanalysis, there is a classic approach to xenophobia and discrimination based on the theory of the imaginary. Segregation, racism, and hatred of the other are based on the problems of narcissism and specularity. There is the conviction that the small differences that characterise each of us mark us out as better than the others. What is rejected in the other comes from the need to protect the coherence of one's own image, to ignore one's own repressed self. Personally, I have come to hold that the Freudian assertion that the self is constituted by expelling the bad, considering it external, as belonging to the not-self, and retaining the good as one's own continues as a conviction throughout life, which leads to considering the self/foreign, native/foreigner, good/bad dualism as natural in later beliefs and convictions.

In the work, "The Uncanny",[4] some clues appear about how what is rejected in the other corresponds to something of its own that is not admitted as such. The word *unheimlich* is subjected to philological scrutiny. The meanings of *heimlich* (familiar, homely, secret) appear mixed with the unfamiliar; thus, the known is transformed into the unknown and strange. In this unsettling strangeness, the repressed that comes back is something that has always been familiar, made strange by the process of repression.

Everyone is a foreigner to their selves, for she or he harbours within her- or himself a vast zone of unknowable otherness, and this unknown other subsists in the relations between individuals, classes, and peoples. Not even in one's own place of origin does one's foreignness disappear. When we discover the terrifying otherness that erupts in the face of the appearance of our own in the other, our self is shocked and shaken. If the foreigner contains the threatening otherness, the bearer of this otherness is eliminated, before it is recognised as one's own. If one succeeds in assuming one's own foreignness, the foreigner ceases to be a threat. This is what makes Julia Kristeva say: "If I am a foreigner, there are no foreigners". The Freudian notion of the unconscious strips the foreign of its pathological aspect and integrates into the human an otherness that becomes an inherent part of its being. The sinister, the foreign, is within us; we are our own foreigner, being irreparably divided.[5]

In the face of the foreigner who is rejected and with whom identification appears, limits and autonomy are lost. This destructuring of the ego can last as a psychotic symptom or result in a new opening. The threatening experience of the disturbing strangeness would be the index of the latency of the psychotic contents, of the fragility of repression, and of the symbolic inconsistency that structures the repressed. In other words, the more fragile the constitution of a subject, the more threatened she or he will feel by the different.

Xenophobia and Prejudice

In the "Project of Psychology",[6] Freud states that "the other, the similar, is the first satisfying object, the first hostile object and the only auxiliary force". Thus, the only possibility of life for the new subject starts from a prior other, external to herself. In order to become a subject, it is essential that she loves and invests in this other. This need of the other for the life and constitution of each subject creates love and also hate. Love from satisfaction, and hate— which increases with frustration—from rivalry, from disagreement.

In this complex web of links, the appearance of a different other who comes from somewhere else and has different habits and beliefs provokes a particular response. The word *foreigner* contains the Greek root *xenos*, and its enunciation expresses the contempt and strangeness aroused by what is considered strange, alien, barbaric, undesirable, although sometimes the stranger may be loved or admired. This difference arouses mistrust and aggressiveness, only overcome by civilisation. But we also know that it is difference that allows love and sexual attraction, and that cultural differences make possible the enrichment of human groups and the broadening of their horizons. With all these differences, given that we humans belong to the same species, which originated in a single place on the planet and today covers it entirely, wherever we are, we have all arrived at our current residence as foreigners.

We are now faced with the problem of prejudice, which is the unconscious part of a society's ideology: the set of feelings, judgements, and attitudes that provoke and justify discriminatory measures, separation, segregation, and exploitation of one group by another.[7]

Racial prejudice is widespread. Today, we understand that race is not defined biologically or anthropologically, but sociologically. Contemporary biology does not support the notion of race because, first of all, although human beings differ from each other in their physical characteristics, for these variations to give rise to clearly delimited groups they would have to coincide with each other, and this is not the case. A first map of "races" would be obtained if genetic characteristics are measured; a second, if blood analysis is measured as a criterion; a third, if it is the bone system; a fourth, if it is the epidermis. On the other hand, within the groups thus constituted, there is a greater distance between the individuals of which they are composed than between the groups themselves. For these reasons, contemporary biology no longer resorts to the notion of race, which is nowadays conceived as a term of social psychology.[8]

Another widespread prejudice is gender bias: women are the first to be discriminated against in all societies. The poor are the second, as indolence and laziness are attributed to them as the cause of their condition. There is also cultural and religious prejudice: when Western Europeans came into contact with America, Africa, or Asia, they considered people there barbarians or savages, and today, in the 21st century, the different fundamentalisms put the world in danger of extinction. Roger Bastide believes that ignorance is involved in the birth of prejudice, and that economic, political, and sociological factors contribute to its constitution. Prejudice is also linked to the authoritarian and rigid personality, which cannot adapt to changing social structures.

Racism and hatred of the foreigner are universal features of human societies: it is the impossibility of being constituted without excluding, devaluing, and hating the other.

Hanna Arendt considers it abominable to hate the other for what she or he is not responsible for, such as his or her belonging to a certain race, but this is the essence of racist prejudice, for which no abjuration is possible.[9] Racism does not desire the abjuration of the other, but his or her death and extinction.

Walter Benjamin identifies the inner representation of the foreigner with a deformed figure from fairy tales and nursery rhymes: the little hunchback.[10] This figure is an *unheimlich* being, the children's bogeyman, a supplement, a dangerous leftover from society.

The creation of the other or the deposition of certain characters in the other stems from the need to protect the coherence of one's own image. For example, Roger Bartra argues that the creation of the myth of the savage man is a fundamental ingredient of European culture, the creation of an alter ego, an artificial savage who preserves the identity of the European as a civilised Western man.[11]

The archaic, narcissistic self, not yet delimited from the outside, projects outside it what it experiences in itself as dangerous, turning it into a strange or demonic double.

Thus, an authoritarian community uses only one brain: that of the leader. In a democratic one, on the other hand, all brains can function in parallel. Authoritarianism is a cognitive poverty incompatible with the demands of the 21st century.

In this sense, the xenophobic ideology tries to rescue an omnipotent and archaic identity ideal, a compact and immutable identity through time and history, proclaiming a glorious, immaculate past, which the foreigner would come to disturb. Racist ideologies develop in those who suffer from poverty, unemployment, and hopelessness, who thus avoid questioning their own grief and uncertainty.[12]

Prejudice Fostered

Our social subjectivity comes from our biography, from our family and social insertion, from the identifications that take place in childhood but also throughout life. Guilt at disidentifying from parental or community beliefs leads to the fear of isolation, as well as the loss of connection and belonging to family and society.

Prejudice is linked to what Freud states in *Psychology of the Masses and Analysis of the Ego*,[13] where he argues that the existence of a leader with power and charisma has effects of identification and hypnosis. The subjects grouped around the leader identify with each other and place the ideal of the self in the admired leader, a behaviour that satisfies a narcissistic need: to be as exalted and powerful as he is. If they are equal to the admired leader, they are narcissistically perfect, identifiable with the ideal; they suffer no faults. Likewise, sharing beliefs and convictions with their peers gives them a feeling of belonging that is of the utmost importance for the psychic economy.

Thus, the concept of belonging refers to an unconscious and unavoidable *imprinting*. This value, prior to one's own experience, may or may not be appropriate; it may always be there as an unquestioned mental substratum, as a given, or it may become conflictive and make change possible. The prejudices and beliefs of each human group give a sense of belonging and identity to that community, which is essential, to the point that the members of these groups can adopt an incredible behaviour in order to be accepted and not lose this belonging; otherwise, it would be unthinkable that an ordinary person would commit Nazi crimes.

The concept of belonging and adapting to anything in order to maintain it has some bearing on Arendt's ideas about the banality of evil.[14] Indeed, Arendt describes Eichmann as an ordinary person who is completely incapable of distinguishing the good from the demonic and of developing any personal thought. His entire language consists of clichés, so that his phrases appear as an example of the manipulation of individuals by totalitarian regimes. Characters such as Eichmann do not think and they are not autonomous; they are incapable of judgement, as they execute the directives of others, but by this behaviour they decide who lives or dies. Eichmann was guilty because he had obeyed, but he regarded obedience as a virtue that made him one with the powerful.

When differences that can be conceived as ethnocultural are considered innate, indelible marks of inferiority, we find an attitude of racist ideology. Racism sets out to establish a hierarchy of groups that identifies the laws of nature with divine laws. This racism has two components: difference and power; it is a theory that regards others, those different from us, as inferior, with permanent and unchangeable differences. This sense of difference gives a reason to use power as an advantage by treating others in a way that we would consider cruel or unjust if it were applied to members of our own group. The new "cultural racism" that some English sociologists have described holds that the characteristics of social groups are fixed, natural, and confined in a culturalism that is defined from a given, pseudo-biological perspective. We will see how this is not so.

We generally take it for granted that these situations describe one rich/powerful person discriminating against another who is already poor and powerless. This is a blunder; there were no poor human beings 10,000 years ago, before the agrarian revolution. The poverty of the other is caused by the rich or the one who strives to get richer.[15] The same mistake is made in assuming that the rich/intelligent versus poor/dumb intellectual capacity step is already taken for granted. On the contrary, someone becomes poor or dumb because there is an enabler. In ancient Greece, the Lacedaemonians had a very devious way of handling their *ilotas* slaves: they forced them to wear clownish clothes, to get drunk, to commit sexual atrocities between daughters and fathers, until the *ilotas* felt like beasts incapable of reasoning, organising, and rebelling. Now these slaves really had the condition that the Lacedaemonians had attributed to them at the outset. Nat Turner, the famous black American slave who led the only effective rebellion, in August 1831, in Southampton, Virginia, said: "Take a slave, punish him to a rag amid shrieks of pain, and he is yours forever. But don't be given to instructing him, for the first thing he will do is to strangle you". A sad result was that, in the United States, in order to help/compensate its African American citizens, special places were reserved for young African American students in the most prestigious universities, against the preaching and will of the racists, who maintained that it would be useless because African Americans were seen as inferior and could not thrive in such educational institutions. It soon became clear that African Americans had not reached the intellectual level to take advantage of the courses and did not receive the necessary grades. For, while the white students had attended excellent primary schools and secondary schools equipped with all the requirements of a theoretical and practical education, had visited as tourists the places of the world that were mentioned in the lectures (Greece, Egypt, Paris, Rome), had mastered foreign languages, had seen the plays, and knew the authors who were described, the African Americans had perhaps never heard of them. Such results consolidated the prejudices of white racists. This supports our view that rich, powerful, and authoritarian people often use their wealth, power, and authority to inflict poverty, weakness, and injustice on whomever they can.[16] In this sense, discrimination against the poor led the Mexican politician Carlos Hank Gonzalez to say: "A penniless politician is a poor politician".

On the other hand, human beings have been selected for their capacity to be believers, as this gives them the possibility to believe and incorporate into their cognitive heritage not only what each person learns directly, but also what is learned by society as a whole.[17] All human knowledge is incorporated into the cognitive bank through upbringing and education, through the word of parents, family, and teachers, which allows us to be the repositories and continuators of universal knowledge and thought. We inherit knowledge and vital criteria pathognomonic of the society to which we belong, but we also incorporate without scrutiny most of the prejudices that our ancestors have collected through generations.

Social policy, rather than asserting that we are all equal, must work with the idea of tolerating differences. Even if we know that the process underlying prejudice is not rational, we must reinforce the social tools to manage it. In

Brazil, the law that considers any manifestation of racism as a crime is important. It does not prevent the feeling, but it sends the message that it will not be tolerated by the nation/parent.

Finally, we conceive of prejudice as a phenomenon that is embedded in the transgenerational unconscious but depends on the communal and social. The transformation of benign prejudice (preferences, adhesions, awareness of certain differences) into malignant prejudice, which implies destruction and annihilation of those who are different, as has happened in the catastrophes of the 20th and 21st centuries, depends on political, social, and economic factors, so that its comprehensive study is interdisciplinary.

Prejudice and Psychoanalysis

Sociology is, so far, the discipline that has been able to provide the most accurate conceptions of prejudice. Psychoanalysts must specify the psychodynamics of prejudice, in the individual, in institutions, and in societies. This would allow us to understand the difficulties arising from the psychoanalyst's own prejudices during treatment and to think about how to elaborate work on the patient's prejudices. We have seen prejudice as the acceptance or rejection of differences, as the narcissism of small differences, or as a defensive mechanism to deny them.[18]

Thus, we will raise some considerations:

a   the production of prejudice and the psychic monad;
b   the place and management of prejudice in psychoanalytic practice; and
c   some difficulties posed by prejudice for the evolution of psychoanalytic theories.

We are going to introduce the theory of the psychic monad proposed by C. Castoriadis,[19] which proposes a hypothesis about the emergence of prejudice in the early self.

The Psychic Monad

The monad is a phase and a mode of functioning that can characterise all psychic strata (id, ego, superego) and that affects the subject's way of thinking about him- or herself and his or her conception of the functioning of society, as well as of certain cultural formations, such as religion. The monad sustains a totalitarianism, insofar as it ignores everything that is not a product of itself. Its functioning is omnipotence, which gives rise to the omnipotence of thought and the undifferentiation between the self and the external.

When the equilibrium between monadic totalitarianism and its scheme of indistinction breaks down, a state of hallucinatory satisfaction and intense self-hatred tends to be installed in the subject because of the impotence to do and have everything. This hatred is projected on to the other; differentiation begins to take place, and the notion of an external world that is hated because it is not possessed appears. What is foundational for psychic space, according to Castoriadis, is the representation of a desire that is already satisfied, and it is the frustration of this state of satisfaction that begins to introduce the notion of the external world.

The psychic monad transcends the psyche, for it is in search of a unity of tranquillity and fulfilment. Later, it is also present as a search for absolute truth in philosophy and science and leads to the constitution of dogmas and religious sentiments.

From this point of view, the subject always wants to find the original state of tranquillity and certainty in his or her psyche and in the social collective. It is a quest to destroy all differences, to return to a feeling of nirvana; if a difference appears, it is not tolerated and must be destroyed. As a defence against its own impotence and need, hatred is projected outwards—that is, towards the other. This hatred can lead to the emergence of the desire for non-desire, for death. When the monadic closure is broken by the pressure of the body and the other, becoming occurs, and the psyche and the perception of need are generated.

The other will always be the cause of the rupture of the monad and of the hatred projected outwards, which is the origin of the hatred of the other and which, in the last analysis, could be considered as the individual origin, specific to each subject, of prejudice.

For the fall of omnipotence, it is necessary for the other—be it the mother, the father, or society—to disown itself and not to see itself as the origin of all truth and universal knowledge. Otherwise, the chain of omnipotent thought is formed: "I am everything, I have everything, the other is nothing, worthless". In other words, a devaluing and prejudiced conception of the world is enclosed.

Prejudice in Psychoanalytic Practice

For psychoanalysts, prejudice also confronts us with difficulties in our clinical practice, for our theories may function as prejudices that make it difficult for us to listen to the new and the different, in case the patient's discourse contains words that denote an ideology that is adverse to us. We may lose our floating attention and focus excessively on a certain problem. Some prejudices pose a difficulty for the development of our psychoanalytic discipline, and yet we need them as a support for our work. They are epistemological obstacles or limitations to our listening to what is strange to us and making room for the difference of the other, with its unexpected or unknown elements.[20]

As far as the psychoanalytic cure is concerned, we think that it considers the analyst in a dialectical analyst–analysand process and places him or her in a situation of commitment. This way of placing oneself in the treatment recognises the analyst's influence on the analysand's transference,[21] which responds to his or her history and also to the way he or she is expected and listened to. Thus, we consider that prejudice appears both in the analysand's narrative and in the analyst's mind and discourse. It is important to recognise when the analyst's prejudice becomes an obstacle to understanding the content of a session, a situation that impacts on the analyst's countertransference[22] and on the possibilities of listening.

As we have said, the other, with his or her difference and strangeness, shakes our identity certainties, as he or she proposes different approaches to vital questions, beliefs, and convictions. The psychoanalyst is also in this situation when listening to an analysand who has greater or lesser differences from his or her own beliefs and concepts; although the analyst's own analysis gives him the capacity to listen to someone who differs from his own opinions, these differences constitute a problem.

The impossibility of approaching the object of knowledge without pre-existing baggage of criteria and values colours and modulates the analytic relationship and the countertransference. In the psychoanalytic session, pre-judice necessarily appears in the minds of both protagonists, from family beliefs, belongings, theoretical positions, and therapeutic objectives. Conscious or unconscious prejudices operating in the psychoanalyst's mind towards someone who holds other beliefs, other political positions, especially in situations of importance to the former, can result in a countertransferential obstacle to listening to the analysand. In fact, we react with prejudice, with rejection, if only with our feelings, to any idea or characteristic of the patient that does not coincide with our own beliefs, and we must do some elaborative work on these feelings before saying or not saying something.[23]

Thus, every analyst participates in the situation of the cure with his or her psychic presence in the analyst–analysand dialectic, where she or he is the bearer of their onto- and phylogenetic imprint, their *Weltanschauung*, their unconscious Oedipal constellation, subjectivity, values, origin, culture, referential framework, analytic affiliation, own theory of the clinic, beliefs, convictions, and prejudices. This conception of the cure, which includes what is personal in the psychoanalyst as a qualified, marked, and particular response, affects the transference of the analysand, who responds to his or her own history and characteristics. Countertransferential responses have long been understood as exclusively caused by the analysand's associative activity or performance, but a more inclusive conception of the role of each participant in the analytic process allows us to conceive them as part of the analyst's internal framework, of his or her own elaborative work and personal variables. Likewise, it makes us see that our listening and our conscious or unconscious attitude of acceptance or rejection enable or hinder the analysand's speech.

The notion of the analytic field[24] holds that the intersubjectivity present in the analyst–analysand duo exceeds the concepts of transference and coun-tertransference, as these are thought of as individual phenomena that occur in the patient and the analyst separately. The concept of field implies a constant oscillatory tension between the individualities of each within the intersubjective field.

We will now consider the place of neutrality and abstinence between objectivity, subjectivity, and intersubjectivity. Claudio Eizirik thinks that the question of analytic neutrality is central and considers that it is still a useful concept, although it needs to be updated and revitalised.[25] He suggests a position in which the analyst retains the necessary empathy, maintaining a possible distance in relation to the patient's material and transference, the countertransference and his or her own personality, as well as in relation to his or her own values, the expectations and pressures of the external world, and psychoanalytic theory. From this factor, he postulates a certain possible distance, necessary to allow the emergence of the analysand's desire and conviction. We can add that our own convictions, prejudices, and theories that are inherent in us, such as our judgement, are present in the analytic situation, but that being aware of this allows us to favour, to leave space for, the emergence of the analysand's thought and desire. What we need is to find a mode of communication that opens up the analysand's personal perspectives, that does not close his or her ways but expands them. Perhaps this is neutrality: not offering or suggesting the route to follow, but accompanying the analysand in his or her search.

Prejudice and Narcissistic Transference

Scientific disciplines change with use, so that none of them is today exactly as its pioneers formulated it. Psychoanalysis, throughout its evolution, has undergone remarkable theoretical and clinical changes, such as those introduced by Klein, Lacan, post-Kleinian authors such as Bion, Meltzer, and others, but prejudices have also arisen that tend to turn it into a discipline that distances itself from the importance of unconscious determinations and that tries to reduce it to an objective cognitive science, akin to psychiatry, reductionist and parochial.

Obviously, the above-mentioned changes and positions somehow intervene in the training of new psychoanalysts, which is the subject of this section.

With respect to psychoanalysis, it is worth noting the importance of the way in which the transmission of psychoanalytic knowledge takes place and the conditions under which the analyst–analysand relationship, which we call transference, is established, for, if this is handled in an authoritarian manner, the whole process can lead to theoretical immobilism. In such a case, what underlies this authoritarian form is the narcissistic belief in the analyst's knowledge, a belief that is held by both the analyst and the analysand (candidate analyst) and does not allow access to anything that questions this knowledge.

The fact that the practice of psychoanalysis is made possible by the analyst's analysis creates particular conditions in the transmission – that is, in the training of the analyst – as well as in the structure of psychoanalytic associations. Hence, if we maintain that what is desirable is that the young person in training identifies with his or her psychoanalyst, we must bear in mind that transference can favour authoritarianism and single-mindedness.

Authoritarian situations coming from psychoanalytic institutions can occur in the different links established in the transmission of knowledge – didactic analyses, supervision, seminars – as well as in the wider institutional setting. Often, there is an idealising/idealised, dominant/dominated commitment that stems from a double need on the part of the analyst, who thus denies the lack[26] and the necessary passage to his or her symbolic death. The same happens on the analysand's side, for, if he denies the death of the father, he also denies his own death and his own castration. Therefore, it is not a unilateral situation, but a shared pathology.

To illustrate these situations, we will quote from a paper by Siegfried Bernfeld in which he states that, although the first didactic analyses were conducted informally by Freud, advising or interpreting the dreams of his analysands, the formalisation and institutionalisation of analysis and training were imposed after 1923. According to Bernfeld, this was the moment after Freud became aware of the life-threatening danger of his illness, which was later exchanged for a more benign prognosis that gave him several more years to live.[27]

The desire to take the place of the dead father and the repression of this desire, says Bernfeld, resulted in a sterilising administrative severity and rigidity, tending to deny parricidal desires and to reproduce the superegoic prohibitions for children and siblings. It was decided, then, to rigidly limit all admissions and to establish coercive and authoritarian training, punishing the disciples for their own ambivalence. In other words, a bureaucratic measure was taken to cover up the desire for the father's death. We can attribute to this kind of situation the rarefication of the analytic atmosphere and attribute to the various phenomena that take place in the group of psychoanalysts causes that go beyond conscious desires.

Thus, in addition to the conflicts inherent in all institutions, such as sibling rivalries and jealousies, idealisation of the leader, and intensification of basic emotions, there are those arising from the constant permeation of transference, often used to favour authoritarianism on the one hand and imitation and sub-ordination on the other. This gives rise to Carl Jung's phrase, who in March 1912 invokes Zarathustra and writes to Freud: "One rewards a master poorly if he only remains a disciple".[28]

In the cure, the analysis of the transference allows the lifting of phantasms, but the transferential relation between analyst and analysand must not be used in the external or institutional reality. It is in this passage from the transferential content to relations external to the cure that the difficult and ambiguous character of psychoanalytic partnerships is imprinted.

The fact that Freud uses the term *savage horde* to denote the group of his supporters is related to what he says in "Totem and Taboo": "The children kill each other to take the place of the father".[29] This situation also depends on the characteristics of the father. Indeed, there could be different bond configurations depending on the characteristics of the leader. If, instead of an authoritarian leader, there was a democratic leader, the fate might be different, as the myth assumes that, after the death of the father, the children come to tolerate each other in order to avoid fighting each other to the point of killing each other. Thus, in the article "The Burial of the Oedipus Complex",[30] Freud describes a father who responds to the law, who allows for the growth and appropriation of life by the son.

Other Developments

The possibilities for the analysand to speak his or her truth depend not only on him or her but also on the analyst being able to listen to him or her. By refusing to be the one to rescue the analysand from loneliness and uncertainty, the analyst will emerge to differentiate between the real and the symbolic function she or he assumes.

The analyst does not occupy the place of the object desired by the analysand; he or she can represent it, but it is necessary for him or her to untie him- or herself from this phantasm of being the necessary object in the analytic situation.

The creation of the subject-supposed-to-know[31] rests on the demand of the analysand who seeks to be loved, confirmed in his or her being by the one who possesses this knowledge and provides him or her with an ultimate truth about him- or herself. This presumption of truth and knowledge attributed to the analyst is the driving force of the transference, which provides the illusion of finding someone who guarantees the certainty of the senses found and who hides the irremediable emptiness of the lack of being.

The transference, then, confers on the analyst a faith that is the product of love and that makes him or her occupy the place of the loved object, as the analysand assumes that the analyst possesses what he or she lacks. In analytic work, this faith must lead to questioning.

Both external and internal conditions can lead to the analysand becoming alienated in the analyst's knowledge and willing to trust in advance any word coming from the analyst. It is this trust *in advance* that constitutes faith or maintained transference: whatever happens, there is someone who is infallible, who knows everything. But, if this aspect of the transference is worked on, the analysand will no longer trust anyone's word in advance, although she or he may accept it merely as a hypothesis to be tested. In François Roustang's terms,[32] faith in advance is the delusion always supposed to achieve a new, complete, and saturated rationality, but it is a faith that must be lost. So much so that Piera Aulagnier claims that the possibility of doubting the analyst's word is as important for thought as the discovery of the difference between the sexes is in childhood.[33]

Psychoanalysis is not a heritage regulated by texts and documents. This creates a legal morality, a fiction of certainty, because authentic followers appear, those of exact syntheses. Psychoanalysis should not be transmitted out of loyalty to the parent or by imitation. So, we must ask ourselves why institutions exist. What sustains us in the institution is the need to belong and to affirm, enrich, question, contrast, and expand the theory, the knowledge, the legacy of the parents, and the constitution of sibling bonds.

As Guillermo Ferschtut argues,[34] in certain cases it happens that, instead of the institution existing in the service of the theory that defines the group, it is the institution that appears as the source of identity. In this case, it will be risky to modify the theory because any modification will be perceived as an attack on the institution. Instead of supporting the development of the theory, the institution becomes an end in itself. Such a reversal of the ends is defended as a necessity in terms of safeguarding the institutional identity in which the institution itself becomes paramount: what is obligatory is loyalty to membership – that is, "to fly the flag".

In the face of positions that promote stagnation in the transmission of psychoanalysis, Castoriadis introduces dimensions that were excluded from it, such as the social-historical, imagination, and thought. In contemporary psychoanalytic thought, there persists a predominance of a rationalist and scientistic ideology. This conception identifies thinking with hypothetico-deductive logical reasoning supported by formal logic. This is the perspective of rationalism that underpins the sciences from the Renaissance onwards and is consolidated in the Enlightenment. This position proposes that scientists should demonstrate and justify their theories exclusively on rational bases and from deterministic approaches.

Today, we tend to admit that the unconscious and creative component is very important in the formulation of scientific hypotheses and theories, especially in the context of discovery.

The investiture of the self as the source of creation and the motor of the activity of thought is fundamental, and it requires a process of disalienation and autonomy. Thought appears as a limitless interrogation, something that accepts closure, an instant of arrest of thought for arriving at a momentary truth, but knowing that it will suffer a rupture if the activity of thought does not stop. For this thought, the object sought is the search itself: not the knowledge acquired once and for all, but the love of knowledge. This is incompatible with acquired knowledge, rigidly transmitted and unchangeable.

The possibility of reflection is based on a representative activity of being able to see oneself and act without certainty: this implies a capacity to put in abeyance the rules, the ultimate axioms, that found thought as a conscious activity, with the conviction that other concepts and criteria will be able to replace them.

Thus, the possibility of the subject's own discourse appears when the discourse of the Other has been denied, not necessarily in its content but insofar as it is the discourse of the Other. There must be an elaboration of this discourse that makes it one's own, which is impossible in situations of dependence and subjection to an instituted thought.

This questioning of determinism also leads us to think that, although history exists, it is neither complete nor determinant for the subject, as it is a history that the subject could change with his or her own elaboration and the activity of the analyst. Just as there was a passive subject of history, at the moment of analysis, there is the possibility of an active appropriation: of becoming a subject of history and not being subject to it.

In this sense, it is necessary to rescue the place of elaboration, creation, and historicisation; determinism has a place, but it does not fill everything, otherwise creation and change would be unthinkable. The historical truth of the subject is built on what remains and is reinterpreted from the mnemic traces, and it constitutes the basis for new symbolisations and new meanings.

Notes

1 Cornelius Castoriadis, 1985.
2 Janine Puget, 2009a.
3 Tveztan Todorov, 1989.
4 Sigmund Freud, "The Uncanny", 1986.
5 Julia Kristeva, 1988.
6 S. Freud, "Project of Psychology", 1986.
7 Roger Bastide, 1969.
8 Fanny Blanck-Cereijido and Pablo Yankelevich, 2003.
9 Hannah Arendt, 1973.
10 Walter Benjamín, 1974.
11 Roger Bartra, 1992.
12 Edmundo Gómez Mango, 1998.
13 S. Freud, "Mass Psychology and Analysis of the Ego", 1986.
14 Silvia Amati-Sas, 2000.
15 Marcelino Cereijido, 2011.
16 "We poor and ignorant human beings handle the need to possess things that this organisation of the world imposes on us, like a murderous sword that takes its first victim precisely in solidarity", Catalina A. Rotunno, personal communication.
17 M. Cereijido, 2011.
18 J. Puget, 2009b.
19 C. Castoriadis, 1985.
20 J. Puget, 2009a.
21 A term progressively introduced by Freud, between 1900 and 1909, to designate a constitutive process of the psychoanalytic cure, whereby the analysand's unconscious desires concerning external objects are repeated within the analytic relationship, with the person of the analyst placed in the position of these various objects.
22 From a classical point of view in psychoanalytic theory, countertransference is considered as the set of manifestations of the analyst's unconscious related to the patient's transference.
23 F. Blanck-Cereijido, 2009.
24 Willy Baranger, 1993.
25 Claudio Eizirik, 2002.

26 In psychoanalysis, the lack is referring to a lack of omnipotence, of plenitude, of immortality that afflicts the entire human race.
27 Siegfried Bernfeld, 1962.
28 Carl Jung, 2000.
29 S. Freud, "Totem and Taboo", 1986.
30 S. Freud, "The Burial of the Oedipus Complex", 1986.
31 Subject-supposed-to-know is the way the patient imagines his analyst: the one who knows.
32 François Roustang, 1980.
33 See Luis Hornstein et al, 1991.
34 Guillermo Ferschtut, 2002.

References

Amati-Sas, Silvia, "La interpretación en el trans-subjetivo" (Interpretation in the trans-subjective), in *Revista de Psicoanálisis* (Journal of Psychoanalysis), no. 1, 2000.

Arendt, Hannah, *The Origins of Totalitarianism*, Orlando, FL: Harcourt Brace Jovanovich, 1973.

Baranger, Willy, *Problemas del campo psicoanalítico* (Problems of the psychoanalytic field), Buenos Aires: Kargieman, 1993, pp. 129–164.

Bartra, Roger, *El salvaje en el espejo* (The savage in the mirror), Mexico: Era, 1992.

Bastide, Roger, *El prójimo y el extraño* (The neighbour and the stranger), Buenos Aires: Amorrortu, 1969.

Benjamín, Walter, *Reflexiones sobre niños, juguetes, libros infantiles, jóvenes y educación* (Thoughts on children, toys, children's books, youth and education), Buenos Aires: Nueva Visión, 1974.

Bernfeld, Siegfried, "On Training Analysis", *Psychoanalytic Quarterly*, no. 34, 1962, pp. 115–144.

Blanck-Cereijido, Fanny, Panel on Prejudice. IPA Committee on Prejudice (including anti-Semitism), Working Group, 2009.

Blanck-Cereijido, Fanny and Yankelevich, Pablo (Eds.), *El otro, el extranjero* (The other, the foreigner), Buenos Aires: Libros del Zorzal, 2003.

Castoriadis, Cornelius, "Reflexiones en torno al racismo" (Reflections on racism), in *Memoirs of the Colloquium "Unconscious and Social Change"*, Paris: Association pour la recherche et l'intervention psychologique, 1985.

Cereijido, Marcelino, *Hacia una teoría general sobre los hijos de puta* (Towards a General Theory on Sons of Bitches), Mexico: Tusquets, 2011.

Eizirik, Claudio, "Entre la objetividad, la subjetividad y la intersubjetividad: ¿Aún hay lugar para la neutralidad analítica" (Between objectivity, subjectivity and inter-subjectivity: is there still a place for analytical neutrality?), *Aperturas Psicoanalíticas*, 12, 2002, www.aperturas.org

Ferschtut, Guillermo, "De los siete anillos a la cadena infinita" (From the seven rings to the infinite chain), *Revista de Psicoanálisis*, vol. 24, no. 1–2, 2002, pp. 267–293.

Freud, Sigmund, "Mass Psychology and Analysis of the Ego", in *Collected Works*, vol. XVIII, trans. José L. Etcheverry, Buenos Aires: Amorrortu, 1986, pp. 63–136.

Freud, Sigmund, "Project of Psychology", in *Collected Works*, vol. I, trans. José L. Etcheverry, Buenos Aires: Amorrortu, 1986, pp. 323–436.

Freud, Sigmund, "The Burial of the Oedipus Complex", in *Collected Works*, vol. XIX, trans. José L. Etcheverry, Buenos Aires: Amorrortu, 1986, pp. 177–187.

Freud, Sigmund, "The Uncanny", in *Collected Works*, vol. XVII, trans. José L. Etcheverry, Buenos Aires: Amorrortu, 1986, pp. 215–251.

S. Freud, "Totem and Taboo", in *Collected Works*, vol. XIII, trans. José L. Etcheverry, Buenos Aires: Amorrortu, 1986, pp. 1–162.

Gómez Mango, Edmundo, "La identidad abierta" (The open identity), in M. Viñar (Ed.), *¿Semejante o enemigo?* (Friend or foe?), Montevideo: Trilce, 1998.

Hornstein, Luis, et al., *Cuerpo, Historia, Interpretación. Piera Aulagnier: de lo originario al proyecto identificatorio* (Body, history, interpretation. Piera Aulagnier: from the original to the identifying project), Buenos Aires: Paidós, 1991.

Jung, Carl, "Freud and psychoanalysis", in *Complete Works*, vol. 4, Madrid: Trotta, 2000, pp. 87–214.

Kristeva, Julia, *Étrangers à nous-même*, Paris: Fayard, 1988.

Puget, Janine, Correspondance, IPA Committee on Prejudice (including anti-Semitism), Working Group, 2009a.

Puget, Janine, *Los prejuicios como instrumentos* (Prejudice as an Instrument of Discrimination), Buenos Aires: APdeBA, 2009b.

Roustang, François, *Un funesto destino* (A dismal destiny), Mexico: Premia, 1980.

Todorov, Tveztan, *Nous et les autres*, Paris: Seuil, 1989.

Chapter 4

The Obviousness of Prejudice, an Unavoidable Transcultural Problem

Silvia Amati Sas

From an etymological point of view, the linguists tells us that "obvious" comes from the Latin *obvius* and from the verb *obviare*, from *via* (route), the way everyone can find clear, manifest, evident. The dictionary definition of "to obviate" is to anticipate, prevent or eliminate difficulties by effective measures. Putting these ideas together, we can say that we see as "obvious" a common way (that each person thinks that everybody takes) to avoid something negative.

We can consider "obviousness" as a background to subjective life, as a necessary illusion of the complementarity of contexts where uncertainties and primitive catastrophic anxieties are deposed and immobilised, outside oneself (Freud, 1919; Bleger, 1967). We are in the realm of Sandler's "background of safety" (Sandler, 1959), the necessary feeling of the coincidence of the subject's perceptions with those of a whole; an illusion of familiarity with the spatio-temporal and affective environment, which makes it appear evident, "natural", taken for granted! This profound and naïve expectation makes the complementarity of contexts with ourselves so much taken for granted that, when a subject is placed in extreme conditions, he/she becomes able to "adapt to whatsoever" (Amati Sas, 1989) – that is, to consider as obvious even the most degrading and dangerous circumstances, which become familiar even if, paradoxically, they are profoundly disturbing. We can see that, at a certain psychic level, we incorporate the context with no choice, or conflict. This does not mean that we deny reality; on the contrary, it rather seems to be an introjection of reality such as it is (for example, the victims of an earthquake settle in the new reality, incorporating themselves into the context); catastrophic news (earthquakes, a boat sinking, bomb explosions), which provoke one's perplexity, a day later become something obvious in the trans-subjective and common perception of reality (and this is accentuated today by the undifferentiating style of mass media; Amati Sas, 2010).

Manipulation of social contexts aimed at the acquisition of power (through terror propaganda or other types of traumatic violence) influences, without people being aware of it, the shared need for certainties.

The use and abuse of social manipulation (through mass media, for example) have become tacitly accepted, and, therefore, it is not easy to deal with

DOI: 10.4324/9781003291978-5

the social conformism they generate. For instance, with reference to foreigners (immigrants), we may easily incorporate a climate of xenophobic propaganda, which, as historical experience shows, can degenerate into dangerous racist or ethnocentric prejudice.

The "prejudice about the stranger" is a trans-subjective phenomenon that can be found anywhere, in all cultures and traditions, and can be easily spread in a mass culture. In a transcultural IPA working group, in which I have participated, we have unanimously agreed on prejudice being universally present in every person's mind.

Prejudices are linked to "belongings", either to some abstract belonging (ideological, religious) or to the concrete participation in different kinds of belongings (family, clan, tribe, country etc.). Prejudice as a form of thought belongs to the order of "preconceptions" that have not yet become judgements. Many prejudices are "convictions" that will not easily develop into critical thought. We can "think through thoughts, or think through convictions" says Berenstein (1986). When we think through convictions, we ignore the existence of conflict or doubt, or that someone else might think differently. These two ways of thinking coexist in each subject and, necessarily, in an intersubjective dialogue.

The origin of prejudice in child development can be related to the so-called "eighth-month anxiety", or "stranger's anxiety", which could be a first observable sign of the feeling of belonging to the familial group, in relation to some other situated "outside" it.

The "eighth-month stranger" becomes the exquisite bearer (or depositary) of what is unknown and new to the baby, in whom it provokes perplexity, amazement, estrangement and also curiosity, the expectation being either to recognise the other as similar or discover someone different. This emotional signal connected with the discovery of the other situated outside the family offers a psychic organiser in evolution. From there on starts a repetitive process in constant transformation that concerns self-continuity in relation to the others outside the familiar self.

What may be expressed, at an object relation level, as an aspect of the process of "separation/individuation" becomes, in the realm of belonging, a sense of inclusion or exclusion of the other. Exclusion can be established in the child as a prejudice if the family attributes negative qualities to the "stranger" (such as dirtiness, ugliness or aggression).

The word "stranger", despite having the same etymological root as "strange", belongs to the field of the representable, thinkable or what can be symbolised (much as the idea of family), whereas "strange" implies primary affective signs such as fear of becoming undifferentiated, fear of losing one's identity integration, "fear of breakdown" (Winnicott, 1974), "nameless dread" (Bion, 1962/1967), *perturbante*", "ominous", uncanny.

Social prejudices such as racism or anti-Semitism are historically determined and derive from public decisions of exclusion, taken by institutional powers. As an example, we may take the categorisation of the Jews as "infamous", made by the Church in the Middle Ages, through edicts in which they were compared to criminals, paedophiles and so on. As the historian Todeschini tells us, the infamous were excluded from society; they had "no fame", which meant no belonging. The institutional origin of these arbitrary concepts is lost in the mists of time, but they are handed down as actual convictions.

We can consider the great collective prejudices to be "containers" (depositaries) of arbitrary and perturbing ideas, which are taken as "obvious" certainties.

We psychoanalysts are immersed, as much as our patients, in a mass-mediated society that has an influence on everybody as well. How can we keep enough concern and alarm in social facts as to usefully include them in our analytical thinking, dialogue and interpretation.

About Psychoanalytic Neutrality

The "psychoanalytical distance", foreseen as a position of neutrality, may lead to the adoption of trivialising attitudes of defensive ambiguity caused by the fear either of open conflict or of an ideological compromise with the patient.

In any case, a suggested technical position of neutrality must not prevent us from thinking, because, if psychoanalytic neutrality should turn into prejudice (conscious or unconscious), this could induce us to "turn a blind eye" (Steiner, 1985) and to accept as obvious or evident thoughts and behaviours that are ethically unacceptable.

Can we add "nor prejudice" to Bion's statement: "not memory, nor desire" (1988)? Thus, psychoanalytic neutrality may not only consist of the indication of "suspending judgement", but also of "suspending prejudice" – an even more difficult claim than Bion's!

To understand how much the context of the present social reality is included in ourselves, as much as we are included in it, we need to widen the criteria pertaining to the intrapsychic and intersubjective world to those concerning the group, or shared subjectivity (trans-subjectivity); this does not imply giving up the classic transferal interpretations of the infantile unconscious past: it is, instead, a matter of more solidly observing the present and the actual preconscious socio-cultural shared reality.

I began to be interested in this problem in relation to patients who suffered consequences of political violence, where a classic psychoanalytic theory did not sufficiently help my understanding and interpretation. I discovered a useful, dynamic way of understanding through José Bleger's model (1967), which explains our subjective dependence on contexts (objects, institutions etc.).

Bleger's concepts of ambiguity and "deposit of ambiguity" in the external context or life's frame can be applied to the comprehension of the psychodynamics of socio-political violence and also of other forms of violence perpetrated within families and institutions.

"Ambiguity" is the clinical expression of an "ambiguous nucleus", a residue of a "primary indifferentiation" that remains within the mature personality. Bleger's sound premise is that this "agglutinated nucleus of indiscriminate contents" cannot be supported by the more mature ego, and, therefore, it is projected and deposited in external "depositaries", through a "symbiotic link".

We can imagine the ambiguous nucleus as a mass of existential uncertainty, non-differentiation and indefinition that is projected and deposited outside the self, determining an obligatory unconscious dependence on external objects, contexts or institutions. This dependence gives feelings of safety and belonging to the subject.

When the external depositaries of the "agglutinated or ambiguous nucleus" are altered or lost (owing to natural or provoked causes, such as exile, mourning, inflicted violence etc.), ambiguity, which is left without external support, returns to the ego.

This sudden re-introjection of undifferentiated aspects of oneself provokes different forms and degrees of anxiety (panic, perplexity, estrangement, confusion); straight away, the ego makes a re-projection and deposits this "ambiguous nucleus" on the new situational context. The subjective consequence is an unconscious adaptation, conformance, familiarity and sense of belonging to the new situation.

From a theoretical point of view, Bleger (1967) adds the "ambiguous position" to the two classic Kleinian positions. The ambiguous position is a pre-conflict, pre-schizo-paranoid position, characterised by the accommodation to circumstances and "numbing" of intense affects.

In the intrapsychic dynamics, the ambiguous position is a transitional position, which gives the ego time to find other defences, but also to create new discriminations and antinomies, and, in favourable circumstances, can allow intuition and discovery of new forms of comprehension and expression.

The ambiguous position becomes a "major defence" when external conditions are suddenly and traumatically changed. In these cases, the mimetic, plastic, oscillatory and malleable quality of ambiguity protects, through adaptation, obnubilation and indifference, the rest of the personality, which seems to remain in a "suspended" state, giving it time to activate other mechanisms of defence and resistance. In the case of persistent social violence (both evident and hidden), ambiguity appears as a trans-subjective "state of ambiguity", an alteration in the capability to use critical thinking and alarm mechanisms, what Eigen (1981) called a "diminution of the sense of catastrophe".

In a state of ambiguity, both the subject and the group may become easily penetrable and suggestible by ideological speeches, which can lead to the installation of paranoid convictions and prejudices. I consider that "defence through ambiguity" is a specific reaction to violence, either in the subject or in the group, and provokes what I have called an "adaptation to whatsoever", which may convey social conformism and prejudices.

In any case, everyone has a subjective reaction to conformism; this is experienced as shame, strangeness or the need "to choose how to belong" to a situation (Berenstein and Puget, 1997).

In the psychotherapy of extreme situations, we find that the victim is often concerned by some other person's dignity and destiny: an "object to be saved" (Amati Sas, 1985). I think the "adaptation to whatsoever" and "the object to be saved" are mechanisms of survival (Amati Sas, 2020).

The Three Spaces of Subjectivity

I consider the social space as "included" in the psychic space and, therefore, pertaining to the psychoanalytic field. In the intrapsychic space, the space of object relations, prejudices may appear as antinomies of the schizo-paranoid type, but they are actually convictions of an arbitrary and imprecise sense that appear as certainties to the subject.

In the intersubjective space, prejudice has a preventing function to control fear of exclusion or to protect one's own belongings from external influences (for example, in a couple, the "mother-in-law" prejudice).

In considering intersubjective space, Berenstein and Puget (1997) bring forward some relevant ideas about the always-present diversity of the other, who, beyond identifications and projections, offers by his/her actual presence an irreducible alterity (*otredad, ajenidad*, in Spanish). Briefly, the other's alterity poses the problem of tolerance of diversity, which is the basis of prejudice.

Common and shared aspects of prejudice are situated in the trans-subjective space. At this level, I want to compare two somehow similar "common and shared" mechanisms: the "adaptation to whatsoever" (Amati Sas, 1989), which I have observed in the treatment of victims of violence, and the "denegative pact", as described by Kaës (1989).

The "adaptation to whatsoever" originates in the unconscious, obligatory (without choice) deposit of ambiguity in common shared contexts; the "denegative pact" implies an unconscious sharing by the group of a certain view of reality that leaves aside, or denies, other aspects of reality.

An evident example of these two phenomena, which belong to everybody's experience, is 11 September 2001, when the Twin Towers in New York were destroyed. We can say that, through the mass media, this provoked a universal feeling of estrangement, as if the Twin Towers had become the frame or context of each and everyone's life, all around the world. This peculiar situation refers to the subjective dynamic of contexts, which are perceived only when they abruptly change. On that traumatic occasion, the first moments of estrangement, perplexity and immobility were followed by the need to explain and give sense to that terrifying event.

In this universal, common state of post-traumatic ambiguity, we accepted without question the definition of "a new war" coined by Bush. We can consider this as an unconscious "adaptation to whatsoever" that has the function of a "denegative pact". But what does this deny? It is the denial of a nameless terror, a psychic void that Kaes (1989) calls "radical negativity".

With his definition of the extreme new facts of 11 September as a "new war", Bush offered a definition with already known words that denied the "terrifying novelty" (Arendt, 1953/2009) of the new uncanny situation.

In everyone's acceptance of an old definition for a totally new reality, we can see a "denegative pact" aimed at avoiding the perception of "our adaptation to whatsoever", the unconscious acceptance of things as they are, which is the main consequence of abrupt violence.

Considering the trans-subjective space of subjectivity, we can approach prejudice in relation to belonging and identity. Bleger (1987/2011) describes two different forms of identity: "belonging identity" and "integration identity".

He says that, when the sense of identity is built on one belonging, there is less tendency to consider the existence of other possible belongings and, therefore, more space for prejudice or fanatical convictions and thinking. In contrast, in a more "integrated identity", the subject's coexisting belongings are more elaborated, and there is more tendency towards judgements and less towards convictions and prejudices.

Some prejudices are connected to transgenerational belongings, relevant to family or social class; others are openly ideological or religious; in any case, there are endless possible belongings.

In the psychoanalytic session, interpretation of the patient's belongings is always a subtle problem, as they are constitutive of the narcissistic self. A counter-transfer prejudice may appear in the therapist when some patient belonging is confronted with some susceptible spot in his/her personal identity.

I give here an example of a counter-transfer aspect of prejudice.

In a Latin American panel at the Chicago IPA congress, a psychoanalyst presented a particular counter-transfer situation.

During a psychotherapeutic treatment, a psychoanalyst of Jewish origin (Dr Grinberg of the Mexican Society) found out, to her own surprise, that her patient was the granddaughter of a Nazi who had been a member of Hitler's movement. The psychoanalyst perceived a strong discomfort in herself and was convinced that she had to stop the treatment, feeling that it was impossible for her to carry on the work undertaken. Her dilemma consisted mainly of her Jewish identity and her conviction that it was impossible for her to maintain a psychoanalytic "neutrality". Nonetheless, she faced the ethical conflict related to her being responsible for the continuity of the psychotherapy, which she considered highly necessary to her patient.

The perception of her uneasiness gave her insight into a prejudice of familial origin (as a result of the experience of a previous generation of her family), which she had never before had the opportunity to elaborate from a professional point of view. In spite of her desire to remain neutral, she perceived that she was inclined to share her family's judgement on the Nazis as an insurmountable prejudice with no possible solution.

The concept of analytical neutrality can function as a prejudice that does not allow us to think and may lead to an impasse. However, the analyst's discomfort and sense of responsibility led her to work through her impasse, to find answers and to continue the psychotherapy.

We see that the technical indication of neutrality may be defensively felt as an imposed rule, which does not allow the therapist's free creativity. It is interesting to remember, with J. Sandler, that neutrality is "dynamic and fluctuating" and that it is "continuously lost and recovered". He considers neutrality as "an elastic concept complementing the analyst's fluctuating attention and answering ability".

The clinical example I have reported allows several observations. It is not irrelevant to consider where and in which historical context these kinds of problems arise. At present, a common imperceptible, actual ideology pervades the psychotherapeutic situation; this includes both protagonists' biographies, the general cultural "climate" in the place where they live and even the freedom of thought allowed by that specific historical period. Here, the Nazis–Jews problem is transgenerational for both patient and therapist.

We could discover later that the patient had chosen a Jewish psychoanalyst owing, let us say, to a geographical prejudice, because she considered Jewish therapists more trustworthy, because of their European origin, compared with the local Latin American ones! Quite an entanglement of prejudices!

It may appear obvious that, for a Jew, a German Nazi can be seen as a hostile "other" or, by definition, an enemy or a stranger. But, in this particular case, I think that the psychoanalyst's reaction of estrangement was not caused just by the appearance of the hostile stranger in the session's material but also by the fact that she realised that her own "strange" counter-transference hostility towards the patient's origin was not directly related to the actual therapeutic relation with her but to historical events.

To perceive one's own estrangeness opens up a dilemma: is what we perceive as so obvious and evident fair or unfair, true or untrue, a mere conviction or a real judgement?

The feeling of estrangeness signals the return to the ego of split or removed aspects of ourselves. It signals the return of a magma of traumatic and perturbing memories that have been transmitted through familial traditions, a prejudice that needs to be worked through, a dilemma to be transformed into a conflict that we can think about, discuss and eventually solve. This does not mean that "prejudice" ceases to be ego-syntonic, but rather that it has been recognised and considered in light of its actual consequences so as to allow us to continue thinking and to choose and decide about it.

For this psychoanalyst, the insight of her strange feelings let her to realise the intensity of her own unconscious participation in the prejudice of her familial group and the fact that she had to think and choose a new way to belong to her group of origin.

At the base of this familial prejudice there were the traumatic memories of a huge social disaster, which constitutes, in Yolanda Gampel's opinion, a "background of uncanny", a transgenerationally transmitted perturbing background, where safety is no longer taken for granted, as what has become obvious is the estranging, destroying power of human beings.

However, if we look at the struggle for existence made by the survivors of social calamities, we may see that those victims' main need was to recapture the appearance of normality, the normal aspects of their everyday life; this great effort was being made to spare the next generation, their children, from knowing the catastrophic reality of what humans are capable of doing to other humans. Unfortunately, whatever the effort made to make life seem normal, this does not prevent the transgenerational transmission of uncanny feelings through discourse and ambiguous behaviour (see Faimberg's (1989/ 2005) "generations' telescopage").

The case cited above made me think of my own countertransferential prejudices, when, in the 1970s, I started, against my will, to deal with highly uncanny psychotherapeutic situations.

I remember I asked myself how I could take care of a patient who had been capable of establishing strong emotional ties to her torturer. I guess this was just one of the most usual, obvious moralistic prejudices we may have towards other people's sexual behaviour. But, in dealing with these patients, I went beyond my possible prejudices, first of all considering the cruelty of the torture context and of the methodically inflicted methods of alienation applied by the torturers.

Many years of therapeutic experience with these patients helped me to understand that the familiarity sought by the torturers with their female victims meant an "imposed consent", a specific and sinister treatment directed at woman prisoners to obtain their compromise, in order to test their degree of alienation.

What I have been able to observe during the therapeutic process with these women was their shame, estrangement, confusion and sense of guilt: they felt towards themselves the same cultural prejudices I could perceive in me, because, as extremely strange and paradoxical as it may appear, we tend to judge the most perverse institutionally imposed situations as facts pertaining to normal private life! For this reason, I believe that "contextualisation" is an essential therapeutic problem when we approach our patients' prejudices or our own. There is a psychoanalytic obligation to put psychic facts into their actual context – social cultural, historical and political.

How can we overcome prejudices coming from our familial and cultural superego and acquire the freedom needed to take into due consideration the enormous anomaly of a given experience, instead of focusing only on the sense of guilt and indignity of the victim, which were intentionally provoked to destroy the victim's ideological belonging and moral integrity?

In addition, my exiled patients had to face the meanness and prejudices present in their current environment, as, outside the therapeutic process, the world was not always empathic and supportive of them. Even political movements and human rights organisations are not always able to remove the cultural prejudices that do not allow us to observe sexual abuse with indignation and equanimity.

In the psychotherapy of these patients, I find it essential to be able to understand the perverse context in all its nuances, trying not to mix in our interpretation of the infantile past unconscious as being the origin of the present problems!

This idea can also be applied to other violent situations of manipulated social exclusion, such as mobbing, or other situations with a perverted aim (as, for example, in the case of a patient of mine who had been the victim of a paedophilic organisation aiming to turn its victims into prostitutes).

In these therapies, we neatly follow an "ethics of concern", a preoccupation with the other's existence and destiny, where we need to follow our own indignation.

In the analysis of each victim, we have to challenge the prejudice and misunderstandings that infiltrate everybody's (ourselves included) trans-subjective life (Amati Sas, 1994, 2010). Undoubtedly, we cannot change social reality; we can only help a single person, our patient, to escape the conviction of being forever occupied by his/her perturbing traumatic experience and offer him/her the opportunity to acquire the affective instruments needed to proceed with his/her life and self-analysis.

Let us go back to the problem of the stranger-foreigner (in particular, clandestine immigrants) that concerns the whole of Europe. This problem gets more serious when the stranger who does not possess a permit to stay is declared a delinquent (an infamous) or, even worse, a non-person who can be left adrift just because he/she is a foreigner ("Are we a 'who' or are we a 'what'?", asked H. Arendt)

It may happen, paradoxically, that those who consider it correct to associate clandestine immigration with delinquency may experience some situation in which they recognise in themselves the opposite attitude, and, on the contrary, that others who think they do not have this prejudice might realise they actually do.

Discovering in ourselves an unsuspected prejudice might cause estrangement, but it essentially makes us feel ashamed. Shame implies a subjective conflict in respect to thoughts or attitudes we did not want or did not believe we had (Amati Sas, 1992a). We often do not realise our conflict and ambiguously defend ourselves from these unpleasant affects with a certain degree of indifference (Amati Sas, 1992b).

In anti-foreigner political propaganda, there is a strong anticipation of dangers such as job losses, threat to the territory, possible changes to habits, religion and so on. It is not easy to make thinkable our unconscious participation in collective fears, but these fears influence our behaviour and our opinions more than we believe.

We do not usually talk about our own prejudices and, if we do, we are not willingly listened to, as this would interrupt the *heimlich*, the "safety feeling", the comfortable compromises and "denegative pacts" established with the whole.

On the subject of our own prejudices, I find André Green's opinion interesting, as expressed in an interview granted to Maurice Corcos in 2006, when he said:

> Secretly, I must admit some unpleasant things about myself: sometimes I realise I am a racist. What can I do? Expiate? No ... the only way to cope with racism is to fight in order to obtain laws that prevent from its consequences. Thus, it doesn't matter whether "I love or I do not love" my feelings, since there is a law that protects the people I don't love.
>
> (Corcos and Green, 2006)

I agree with Green in that we must fight to have laws against racism, but I do not think that the eventual existence of such laws may solve the subjective problem caused by our prejudices towards others or others' prejudices towards us. Instead, I believe that psychoanalytic observation of these difficult problems in the intimacy of the therapeutic session might open a way to understand the public aspects of prejudice and its manipulations.

References

Amati Sas, S. (1985). Megamuertos: Unidad de medida o metafora? *Revista de Psychoanalysis*, 42, 1282–1372.

Amati Sas, S. (1989). Récupérer la honte. In J. Puget, R. Käes et al. (Eds), *Violence d'Etat et Psychanalyse*. Dunod, Paris (*Violenza di Stato e Psicoanalisi*. Gnocchi, Napoli).

Amati Sas, S. (1992a). Ethics and Shame in the Countertransference. *Psychoanalytic Inquiry*, 12, 4, 570–579.

Amati Sas, S. (1992b). Ambiguity as the route to shame. *International Journal of Psychoanalysis*, 73, 329–334.

Amati Sas, S. (1994). Etica e trans-soggettività. *Rivista di Psicoanalisi*, XL.

Amati Sas, S. (2010). La transsubjectivité entre cadre et ambiguïté, in Pichon, M., Vermorel, H., Käes, R. (Eds), *L'expérience du groupe. Approche de l'oeuvre de René Käes*. Dunod, Paris.

Amati Sas, S. (2020). *Ambiguità, conformismo e adattamento alla violenza sociale*. Ed. Franco Angeli, Milan.

Arendt, H. (1953). *Le origini del totalitarismo*. Einaudi, Rome (2009).

Berenstein, I. (1986). *Acerca de las convicciones*. VII Simposio y Congreso Interno APA: El diàlogo analitico II, *Actas*. Buenos Aires.

Berenstein, I. and Puget, J. (1997). *Lo vincular*. Paidos, Buenos Aires.

Bion, W.R. (1962). The psychoanalytical study of thinking. In Bion, W.R. (1967). *Second Thoughts* (pp. 178–186). Heinemann Medical Books, London.

Bion, W.R. (1988). Notes on memory and desire. In Spillius, E.B. (Ed.), *Melanie Klein today: Developments in theory and practice, Vol. 2. Mainly practice* (pp. 17–21). Taylor & Francis/Routledge, London.

Bleger, J. (1967). *Simbiosi e ambiguità*. Ed. Lauretana (1994).

Bleger, J. (1987). Le groupe comme institution. In Kaës, R., *L'institution et les insti-tutions*. Dunod, Paris (2011).

Corcos, M. and Green, A. (2006). *Associations (presque)libres d'un psychanalyste*. Albin Michel, Paris.

Eigen, M. (1981). The area of faith in Winnicott, Lacan and Bion. *International Journal of Psychoanalysis*, 62, 4, 413–433.

Faimberg, H. (1989). *The countertransference position and the countertransference*. In *The Telescoping of Generations*. Routledge, London and New York (2005).

Freud, S. (1919). Il perturbante. *O.S.F.*, Vol. 9, 81–114.

Kaës, R. (1989). Le pacte dénégatif dans les ensembles transubjectifs. In A. Missenard et al. (Eds), *Le négatif, figures et modalités*. Dunod, Paris.

Sandler, J. (1959). The background of safety. In (1987) *From Safety to Super Ego*. Karnac, London.

Steiner, J. (1985). Turning a blind eye: the cover up for Oedipus. *International Review of Psychoanalysis*, 12, 161.

Winnicott, D.W. (1974). Fear of breakdown. *International Review of Psycho-Analysis*, 1, 103–107.

Chapter 5

Prejudice and Its Effects on the Psychoanalytic Clinic

Miriam Grynberg Robinson

In the psychoanalytic process, it is essential that the analyst constantly strives to be aware of his or her own prejudices, both in the transfer relationship and thinking, as prejudice undermines the possibilities of new discoveries and new creative insights.

As analysts, in each analytic adventure we must dare to deconstruct our own prejudices and allow ourselves to enter into the enigmatic, doubtful space of each one, as only then will the patient see that it is possible to take the risk of debating and confronting him- or herself in order to become aware of the prejudices that inhabit him or her and to work with them.

In our psychoanalytic work, the pretence of neutrality is an illusion, as it is not difficult to recognise that most of our assessments are clearly impregnated by a prejudiced vision. Prejudice is inherent in human beings but it reaches different dimensions and magnitudes. It ranges from the most harmless to the most serious and sinister, from neurotic repression to psychotic defences (Woscoboinik, 2000).

Prejudice is a true, obvious, non-conflicting premise that dwells within us and that, despite being perceived, cannot easily be represented, reflected upon or made the object of critical thinking (Amati, 2009).

Berenstein (1986) says that one can think with thoughts or one can think with convictions. When we think with convictions, we are talking from prejudice, that is to say, with a true thought, absent of conflict, a way of thinking that points to the archaic and where the other's way of thinking is not accepted. These two ways of thinking coexist in the subject and in the transferential dyad.

Maria Moliner (2007) defines prejudice as "a preconceived idea that misdirects accurate judgement". It is an idea, feeling or opinion, independent of rational judgement, with which it may even coexist.

Prejudices are stereotyped, insofar as they are traces, impressions, moulds of a solid character that refer to thoughts, beliefs and attitudes registered involuntarily and that are repeated without variation, conditioning individual or group behaviour. They constitute true unconscious automatisms.

Thus, prejudice has, on the one hand, the benefit of a facilitating archive, but, on the other hand, it can become the source of serious injustices and

DOI: 10.4324/9781003291978-6

sinister attitudes. By being generalised and simplifying, it facilitates the slide into Manichean approaches such as black/white, good/bad, genius/idiot. And, from here, it can extend to the ever-threatening extremes of bigotry, xenophobia and racism, which can silently appear in our practices if we do not always try to be aware of the personal prejudices in which each of us has constituted ourselves as subjects.

Prejudice from a Psychoanalytical Point of View

The complexity of the unconscious processes of prejudice forces us to try to understand it from a psychoanalytical point of view. We must not forget that the constitution of the subject begins in what Sigmund Freud called, in "The Project" (1878), "the Complex of the Fellow", where the other, the fellow, is the first satisfying object, the first hostile one and the only auxiliary force. Freud marks the only possibility of life for the new subject starting from another prior and external to him or her, whom it is imperative that she or he loves and invests in if she or he is to become a subject. This necessity of the other for the life and constitution of each subject creates love and hate. Love emerges from the imprint left by the satisfying object and will be transcribed in the psyche in representations that will have the sense of the acquaintance, the friend, the partner, the protector. On the other hand, hate will emerge from the imprint left by the hostile object, that part of each of us that feels an original prejudice where the object has harmed us in its absence, in its frustration. This imprint is transformed into representations that will become part of our prejudices. Thus, the stranger, the enemy, the hostile, the foreigner –we will name them in different ways – depends on the subjectivity and the culture in which we are immersed. Therefore, for some, this hostile, foreign object is deposited in the black person; for others, in the Jew, the Nazi, the feminine, madness, and so on. It is that unknown part of each of us that is projected on to the other; it represents the dangerous part that haunts us and that we expel outside, placing it in the other. To find a being similar to us, but at the same time different, generates in us the feeling of the strange, of the chaos of the incomprehensible.

In the work on "The Uncanny", Freud (1919) explains the following: the rejected in the other corresponds to something of one's own that is not admitted as such by the subject. Thus, the known, intimate (Heimlich), is transformed into the unknown unfamiliar and strange (Unheimlich). In the disturbing strangeness, what returns is something that has always been familiar, made strange by the repressive process, so that the sinister, the unknown and strange are within ourselves.

In Freud's work, from his early statement on the "Complex of the Fellow" to the assertion that there is no individual psychology – the thesis that all psychology is social – the other always appears as a rival, partner or adversary model. In his lengthy deliberations on object and narcissistic libido and on patterns of love object choice, there always remains the interweaving of a fine qualitative analysis that makes eloquent the problem of the complexity of the boundary between the self and the other (Viñar, 2003).

This complexity is established through the basic unconscious mechanisms of projection or projective identification and produces the dilemma of the mirror, of the doubles, of the indiscriminate zones where it is not known whether I see you or I see myself, whether I hate you or I hate myself, which can become a dead-end alternative or an insoluble paradox (Viñar, 2003).

Who am I, and who is the other? This question confronts us with the difficulty of assuming the difference, of losing the narcissistic and fusing omnipotence, as assuming the difference consists in assuming the lack: "I am not everything, nor am I one in the other".

This is the complex game of otherness in which the other, the different one, will become, on the one hand, the one who questions me, who threatens me by his or her possible invasion or persecution (enemy), or who, on the other hand, enriches me in his or her difference (friend). We thus understand that, in the bonds, there are two resolutions for the subject. On the one hand, it is only in difference that love, novelty and the discovery of new horizons are allowed. Here, the other is the source of bonds, of presence, of enrichment through difference, but, on the other hand, the second resolution is narcissistic: the ego does not tolerate the disappointment of "not being the master of its own house" (Freud, 1916–17), and so it resists recognising sexual difference, generational difference and otherness. It resists assuming the lack, the castration, the loss of omnipotence.

Only if we manage to assume that we are strangers to ourselves can we overcome the horror of difference and we will be able to process otherness and confront our prejudices. One of the ways to process them is the analytical process.

Prejudice in the Analytical Process

The complexity of the unconscious processes of prejudice imposes on us the need to assume that we do not present ourselves to the patient as a *tabula rasa*, without memory and without desire. We approach the object of knowledge with a pre-existing baggage of criteria and values that colour and modulate the process.

Unconscious biases operating in the analyst's mind can result in a counter-transferential obstacle to the analytic process. This is why we must be alert. It is essential that the analyst has analysed in his or her own analysis that strange part of him- or herself and be ready to analyse the unconscious biases that can arise at any moment in the process.

Prejudice appears in the mind of both the patient and the analyst. Each one brings his or her own scene from the unconscious, his or her Oedipal constellation, cultural and family beliefs, and, in the psychoanalytic world, each one even listens to the patient from his or her theoretical stance and with his or her therapeutic goals. Is it not the case, for example, that, in Kleinian theory, there is a stance that the patient is able to tolerate depressive pain or repair the damage? And, in the Lacanians, is there not a position related to desire and jouissance? It seems to me that, whatever the implicit theory with which we are thinking about our patients' process, our patients inevitably convey the treatment, as well as our own life experiences, our ideologies, our conception of the good/bad, woman/man and so on.

We must try not to live in certainties but allow ourselves to doubt and constantly question our psychoanalytic being and doing.

I believe that the analyst must conduct him- or herself according to the rule of abstinence and stick to the task of guiding the process of the cure along the paths of the transference–countertransference dialectics. Therefore, if the analyst should come across a case in which she or he evaluates the impossibility of abstaining from a moral condemnation of the patient's behaviour, she or he must not accept that case in analysis. She or he must abstain from analysis.

In the 1960s, Aberastury said that he would "never analyse a Nazi". Each one should think with whom she or he is capable of working with without hurting the human being in front of her or him, or otherwise refrain from doing it. Who could – say – work with a torturer? Is it possible to analyse someone who tortures without becoming an accomplice? These situations seem to have clear answers. The problem arises when the patient is already in analysis, and it is not a question of whether or not to accept the case. For example, when a patient has "Nazi behaviours", do you analyse him or her or not? And, in fact, what is meant by analysing him or her? Interpreting him or her? It seems to me that an intervention is necessary to show the patient his or her narcissistic de-objectifications, and that the analyst is another who exists. Here, depending on the patient's discourse, different types of intervention could emerge: you see me as your torturer or you are being my torturer; you are my partner or my rival.

And one more problem: it is important to recognise when the analyst's prejudice becomes an obstacle to understanding the content of the unconscious material, a situation that impacts both on the countertransference and on the possibilities of listening to it. The analyst must be ready to analyse and metabolise the strange part of him- or herself that makes its appearance in the psychoanalytic process.

Imagine a Jewish analyst who lost family members in the camps. We could easily anticipate the conflict he or she faces in having a patient during whose treatment process the family and personal secret that he is the grandson of a Nazi comes to light. The impact on the analyst is so strong that he or she is forced to ask him- or herself whether or not he or she will be able to continue working with him. But what to do if the patient is already in the process? I think that the most important thing at that moment is not to enter into certainties but, with the difficulty that this entails, to allow ourselves to doubt, to reflect in order to question what the qualifier "Nazi's grandson" means, what is behind the stereotypical nature of the term. The Nazi's grandchild might not be the perpetrator but, on the contrary, the victim of history, and just by bearing the transgenerational mark we would be marking him or her with prejudice.

It is difficult, but important, to remember that the analytical function, as Leclaire says, is "to listen to what is not said. It is to work on the margin to reintegrate into the consensus what tends to be expelled" (Viñar, 2003). In this way, an utterance by a patient is not enough for the analyst to establish a hypothesis of who the patient is. Freud warns us that the analytic position is to place oneself in the listening position and transform these strong state-ments into questions to be investigated with the patient. To say "Nazi's grandson", what does it really mean for him? How is he positioned in front of this fact in his history? How much of this history is the patient's personal history, or how much of it is the others inhabiting him? And not to forget, fundamentally, why does he express such a secret in that historical moment of the process? What meaning does it have in the transferential process? When, in my own practice, I found myself trying to answer such questions and facing the difficulties of these circumstances, I decided to elaborate a vignette of the process in order to share and think about the theoretical-clinical concerns and questions of these analytical experiences (Blanck and Grynberg, 2010).

Once, a patient came to my office owing to the enormous anguish of being pregnant with a boy and the occurrence of compulsive thoughts of rejection and abuse and fantasies of killing the future baby. She was a woman of angelic beauty: tall and slim, blonde hair, fair complexion, light eyes, delicate features and with a soft expression, although her gaze was sad. However, when she began to talk about her baby, I felt as if her gaze and expression hardened, transformed and filled with an overflowing rage, her expression turning into a sinister one. During the first sessions, these ominous changes in her expression led me to have countertransference sensations of confusion, of ambiguity. Aline – the patient – spoke of her panic about hurting or killing the future baby, of the shock of feeling this way, of the pain that her husband would not support her in this situation and only judge her. She said that the husband complained that she was only using him to get pregnant (they already had a 2-year-old daughter and were expecting their second baby). The husband said that she had a relationship with their little daughter as if they were one person, so that he felt excluded from the mother–daughter dyad. The patient adored her daughter but did not understand why she wanted her son to disappear. With these recurring themes, the patient did not give me much input to ask questions; the sessions were filled with the same material that seemed to overwhelm her.

In the first interview, we had agreed that we would have about three or four sessions to decide whether we would work together; in the fourth session, she said to me: "I am terrified that you will reject me, the session is about to end and you haven't said anything about whether we will work together or not".

During the sessions, I was overcome with contradictory emotions owing to her radical changes in expression, tone and discourse. I saw a woman suffering heartbreakingly from her current situation, and, at the same time, it was very shocking to see her expression transform from sad and soft to cold and sinister when she talked about how she might abuse her child. I felt paralysed inside. I didn't understand what was wrong with her, I had a constant feeling of confusion. I didn't know what decision to make. I didn't know why she wouldn't allow me into her personal history.

I asked her: "Are you often rejected by others, or is it you who are afraid that your anger will destroy relationships with them, in this case with me or with your unborn child?" She started to cry and answered: "I don't know. I never really approach people; I panic about being rejected. I don't know how this happened; I never ask how I am in the relationship with the other person, I don't dare".

Here, she had dared. I had certainly committed myself to making a decision with her in the third or fourth session. Time was almost up, and I told her that we would talk about it next time, but that I thought it was important that she had allowed herself to express her concern, as perhaps behind her comment was the fear that I would become her abuser by leaving her in uncertainty for more sessions – that is, whether or not I would allow her to be born as my patient, as perhaps she was panicking that she would not be able to allow her baby to be born. She cried a lot that day.

After that therapeutic event, I decided that, although I was not clear about what was going on with her and what was going on with me, I would find out during the process. What I did know was that I sensed a deeply helpless and frightened woman who was crying out for help, fearful that the overflow of her own rage and aggression would lead her to abuse and destroy her child.

What appeared at the beginning of the treatment was the rejection of the masculine and the father as its representative, but, after some time working together, it appeared that, behind the symptom, there was a family secret, a transgenerational history of racist convictions and malign prejudices that left me perplexed. The patient told me how badly she had been abused by her parents; she said to me:

It hurts me a lot to talk about it … My grandparents tell me that they saw that, since I was born, my parents didn't love me. They saw that I didn't grow up, that I looked skinny, that I cried a lot and that every time they arrived, grandma would say: "This girl is hungry, that's why she's crying"; she would feed me and I would immediately calm down. One day they arrived and the same thing happened as always, but this time I soiled my nappy and grandma changed me and saw that I was all blistered, my buttocks were all cracked. She was shocked at the state they had me in and argued with them. My parents said: "We don't care about the girl. We don't care if she dies". Then grandma said: "Let me take the child". They immediately handed me over, saying that I was unbearable.

From that moment on, when my grandmother said I was about ten months old, I lived with them – my grandparents – until I was seven, when my parents said they wanted me back in their house, that I was their child and not the grandparents'. I had to return home, with much suffering. My parents rejected me all my life.

"Do you have any hypothesis as to why your parents rejected you so radically?" There was a deathly silence. "My story is very difficult."

When she looked down and looked at me again, apparently frightened, confused, my sensation was again the same as in the first sessions: of confusion, of being faced with an enigma, with something unsaid. After a long silence, the patient continued:

Look, in my house there is a situation with my grandparents that we never talk about. What happens is that my grandparents and my father are immigrants in Chile.

When she told me this, an icy feeling came over me, and I thought: Chile agreed to protect some Nazis after the war. My indescribable feeling only allowed me to articulate: "Where did they emigrate from?" With difficulty, she answered me: "From Germany"; she looked down and told me:

My grandfather was a Nazi. My father always rejected him for that, and after a few years of emigration, he [the patient's father] fell in love with a Latin American woman. The grandparents were furious: how could he fall in love with someone of the inferior race. He was an Aryan of the superior race and should be paired with someone like him.

The son could not bear to hear them talk like that and continued with the girlfriend, who was a woman with a totally Latin American physiognomy: short, with dark brown hair, black eyes and brown skin. After some time of a war between the father and the grandparents, they told him: "If you want to stay with the bride, you have to leave the house". He left and married the woman.

Some time after the marriage, the father and grandparents reconciled. Despite this, the grandparents mistreated the daughter-in-law throughout her life: they insulted her for her physical appearance, her skin colour, her origin; they hardly spoke to her and constantly humiliated her. The first grandchild inherited the mother's physiognomy, and the grandparents could not stand this: they cursed the son for having dishonoured the family, and the abuse was extended to the grandchild.

It is in this climate that the patient was born. Being born fully Aryan, the rejection received by the parents, by the Aryan grandparents, was deposited on her. Thus, the victims of the grandparents became the patient's torturers.

When I heard this story, I was perplexed, confused, thinking that I did not want this story to repeat itself, and at the same time I asked myself: can I treat the granddaughter of a Nazi, being the daughter and granddaughter of survivors? On the other hand, I had in front of me a woman suffering, begging for help, with whom I had committed myself to work. Treating her seemed impossible, but I had already accepted her for treatment. What to do?

While I was thinking about all this, my ideas and feelings were confused, ambiguous.

"Aren't you Jewish?" she asked. I was speechless. I was silent while I tried to recover.

> I think you are Jewish, because of your surname. And to tell you the truth, I always choose my doctors from a Jewish background.
> Why?
> I don't know, I feel confident with them, I feel that they are people who know how to understand each other's pain and how to help others.

The session had come to an end; I was exhausted, confused, unable to put my feelings in order. I began to think about the case, to see how difficult it would be to leave the patient after having started treatment and, at the same time, how difficult it would be to continue it; the difficulty of being able to become her victimiser or her victim.

I thought: my patient was the one who had been placed as the victim of her family and was desperately seeking help so as not to repeat the fact of being the victimiser of her baby, as had happened to her. Hatred, violence, destruction had already been deposited in this unborn baby; it was an innocent child who was going to carry the history of three generations full of hatred.

This woman wanted to stop the transmission of this destructiveness in her family. This made me think of her in such a way that I felt the possibility of continuing the treatment. I knew that we were both going to have to work deeply on our inner world.

I decided to continue with the case, and we began to work on everything that was deposited in that baby: the mother's confusion, her intolerance of difference, how she had learned that the different person had to be disappeared, humiliated, rejected, tortured.

The patient confessed to me her confusion between the good and the bad in the world. She told me how her grandfather used to go down every evening to a kind of bunker he had built in his house, to drink and cry about Nazi Germany. And she would ask me questions:

> Is grandpa wrong or is my dad wrong? I have never wanted to understand grandfather's political history and what he did in the war. He rescued me but I know he killed and hurt many, including my father, my mother and my brother.

"How can I understand this without going crazy?" I said. She cried a lot and told me: "I don't know what my parents see in me, who do they see?" "Maybe they see your grandfather", I replied. Again, she cried a lot and then continued:

> My parents, I feel they hate me, but I'm beginning to understand that maybe, yes, you're right, they don't hate me but what they see in me, which is him.

We worked a lot on how the parents could not see her, and she would tell me:

> I feel empty of myself, maybe that's why I can't say what my position in life is, my life is a confusion. My life is a confusion: am I my grandparents' daughter, or am I their granddaughter? Am I my father's father, or am I his daughter? Can I see my son and not all of them within him?

Let us begin the analysis of the vignette with the countertransferential impact. The danger for the analyst in the face of a totally unexpected novelty is that, as the stark reality dismantles our securities, we may be tempted to consider them obvious and take an ambiguous countertransferential attitude that "dissolves or immobilises the analytic work" (Amati, 2000).

In this case, I needed to mobilise my inner world; I had to break my certainties and face my doubts, my confusion. Amati (2000) says that, in order to deal with this type of case where a phenomenon of terrorist novelty appears in the treatment, our first move is to recognise this through a countertransferential reaction of confusion and ambiguity; there is a feeling of blindness. This is a risky moment in the treatment, as what happens in the face of the appearance of the sinister, the element of surprise, dislocates the analyst, takes him or her out of his or her observational function and leaves him or her at the mercy of intense regressions. In this case, I needed to mobilise my inner world; I had to break my certainties and face my doubts, my confusion.

So, at first, I accepted not knowing how to resolve the situation, I gave up the omnipotence of clinging to the certainties that come to us when we are faced with such therapeutic challenges. It seems to me essential to make all this effort in order to recover, as soon as possible, the ability to think and to criticise, thus preserving the meaning of our work, and to continue with an intense elaboration on the part of both of us.

To achieve this, we would both have to overcome the silent pacts and the unspeakable aspects of what has been lived, of what has been transmitted, of its displacements, disfigurations and retranscriptions.

Let us move on to the question: how can I treat the granddaughter of a Nazi?

This question seems to hide the difficulty of accepting such a muddled package, as Bleger would say. But it is precisely the acceptance of receiving the "package" that allowed the patient to "use" (as Winnicott understands it) the Jewish therapist (as the surviving victim, as the recipient of her confusion), because it was about the survival of her son, who seemed to represent the Jew, the "innocent" victim, as she herself was. The question opens up the possibility of the secret of the patient's untold, split history. Not only the secret that hides a history of victim–victimiser and generational undifferentiation, where it is not clear who is who and what place each one has in the generational chain, but also the transmission of hatred and the impossibility of Oedipal elaboration, situations that did not allow Aline to renounce omnipotence and gave rise, instead, to an intolerance of generational, sexual and otherness difference.

Haydée Faimberg (1993), through her theorisation, helps us to think about the case. She tells us that, when there are family secrets, alienating identifications can be established in the process of transgenerational transmission. She considers that this type of identification is an alienating identification for the self, insofar as its cause is to be found in the history of the other. The alienated part of the self is identified with the narcissistic logic of the parents, according to which the other is only tolerated to the extent that he or she can establish a pleasurable validation of the self: "Thus, I love, I am, means that the object considered as good is me. I hate, you are, means that the bad object is you". In this way, the child is the object of a tyrannical intrusion not only because she or he is different, but above all, and paradoxically, because their history is linked to the history of their parents and all that they reject in their narcissistic system.

I consider that the patient was a victim of this type of identification, as the parents seemed to expel in her the intolerable hatred they had for the grandparents and deposit it in the daughter, whom they hated and rejected. This formulation corresponds to the unconscious fantasy of the parents' not-self, converted into the alienating identification of the daughter, who became the not-self and, thus defining herself, acquired a negative identity. We see, then, a double movement in this intersubjective plot: expulsion from the traumatic history of the parents and appropriation by the daughter: by submitting herself to an alien power, her ego was split.

The patient would then have identified herself, silently and unconsciously, with the tyrannical intrusion of the history concerning her parents. She would have been left full of confusion, ambiguity, not knowing who was who. She was now afraid of repeating this narcissistic style of relationship with her child, depositing in him the part of hatred that she did not tolerate in herself, so that the child would become the mother's not-self.

The problem with masculinity was partly what had led her to treatment. Aline's first statement was the masculine, which she had condensed and hidden, the problem that later unfolded into different statements about what was not tolerated, about what was strange and had to be rejected, hated.

That is why I think it is the problem with difference that is important. The patient had a transgenerational history where there seemed to be no room for assuming difference. Otherness could only exist in the generational chain as long as it was defined by hatred. Such was her confusion that she was sometimes unable to differentiate between good and bad.

In her own words, let us remember when she said:

> Is grandfather wrong or is it my dad who is wrong? I have never wanted to understand grandfather's political history and what he did in the war. He rescued me but I know he killed and hurt many, including my father, my mother and my brother.

With this, we can see the complicated situation of the patient. The confusion was so severe that her rescuer, the grandfather, was at the same time the victimiser of many. Her rescuer had an evil dimension, which was difficult for her to think about, as, by identifying with him, she was also the bearer of both the rescuing part and the evil part. Deep confusion – maddening. What was she the bearer of?

Despite all this difficulty, one hope with this patient was that she was the only one in the whole family group who had dared to ask for help, to take an outside look at the whole transgenerational conglomerate; she wanted desperately not to repeat the story in her son. Aline was looking for a place where she could stop and transform the devastating transgenerational story she was carrying.

All this leads me to reflect, in the transferential space, on how she sought to establish a transferential link with a Jewish woman, and that, in this framework, there would be the possibility of staging the conflict. Thus, the possibility of repeating the tyrannical history of victim–victimiser intrusion, of confusion between who was who and of ambiguity in the link was established, but also the hope that we could elaborate and metabolise the package that she deposited with me. Possibly, she chose a Jewish analyst with the fantasy that only a woman with those characteristics would experience how difficult it was for her to accept her male child. In other words, it was as difficult for the Jewish analyst to accept the patient as a Nazi's granddaughter, in her uterodivan, as it was for the patient to accept her own child. Moreover, if her analyst managed to pull herself together and metabolise the chaos of "being pregnant in transference with a baby-patient like herself", she would hopefully be able to do so with her own baby as well.

The fact that I managed to relativise my prejudice and tried to overcome the phantasm of repetition in me in its destructive aspect gave her the hope of trying to free herself from the "destructiveness of repetition".

In short, the Nazi–Jewish was the statement that allowed us to work on everything condensed and hidden that the patient brought with her. From there, we were able to unfold the patient's statements in the face of what was not tolerated, of what was different, of what was strange and should be rejected, hated. It was not the male–female, Nazi–Jewish, victim–victimiser problem, but the anguish of helplessness, of the unnameable.

That is why I affirm that, in this case, the fundamental nucleus to work on was the problem of the strange, the unknown within itself, together with the problem of difference, as the terror of the problematic points to the lack of limits between the outside and the inside, alive–dead, good–bad, omnipotence, the terror of defencelessness.

It is the presence of the analyst that allows the patient to search for the causes and meanings left by the marks of transmission, which are integrated and historicised in the life of the subject and his or her lineage.

Helping the patient to tolerate the spaces of reciprocity that have been devastated by a transgenerationally transmitted trauma is a decisive step in the therapeutic encounter. M. Viñar (2008) warns us: "We must return to memory, not to arrive at the shudder of terror, but to reopen the question of who is my fellow". That is why it is important to mend this tear, where the fellow can regain his or her place in order to continue to be human. A person needs his or her fellow in order to be human.

It is necessary to work on the trauma, the prejudice that is produced and its transmission, seeking its elaboration. Elaboration work is a constant path that contains the limits of meaning and meaninglessness within the transferential space.

Despite the psychoanalytic mandate, which is to go in the direction of autonomy of thought, our prejudices could hinder it. Thus, we must be alert to save the independence of the analyst's and the patient's thinking from invasive dehumanisation, and respond to the ethics of responsibility towards the human other. That is why this chapter aims to open up the problematic of which patients we are willing to receive and continue with them in their process.

While I. Berenstein (2004) talks about "making room for the foreignness of the other" and Roustang (quoted by Volnovich, 2003) creates the notion of the "passion for otherness", we must ask ourselves whether we wish to establish an analytical process with all otherness. I believe that there are othernesses that are inadmissible, but there are also othernesses that, despite seeming impossible, may become possible if we manage to keep listening to the tangled history that might lie behind a statement of identity. This can be achieved as long as the analyst maintains a deep responsibility to recognise his or her prejudices and relativise them in pursuit of critical thinking, knowing that, as analysts, we must seek abstinent behaviour, but assuming that we are not neutral.

In the 18th century, Rabbi Baal Shem, the originator of Hasidism, expressed in a beautiful parable the unprejudiced aspect of the human being. He said: "The individual is not a cog in a monstrous machine; it is up to him to modify even the laws that imprison him."

References

Amati, S. (2000). "La interpretación en lo transubjetivo. Reflexiones sobre la ambigüedad y los espacios psíquicos" (Interpretation in the transubjective. Reflections on ambiguity and psychic spaces). *Revista de Psicoanálisis*, 57, 1, 129–139. Buenos Aires.

Amati, S. (2009). "La obviedad del prejuicio" (The obviousness of prejudice). Lecture presented at the Foreign/Family Congress. Milan Centre for Psychoanalysis, Milan.

Berenstein, I. (1986). "Acerca de las convicciones" (About convictions). *Actas del Vlll Simposium y Congreso Interno de Apdeba.* Asociación Psicoanalítica de Buenos Aires.

Berenstein, I. (2004). *Devenir otro con otro(s) ajenidad, presencia, interferencia.* (Becoming other with other(s) otherness, presence, interference). Ed. Paidos, Buenos Aires.

Blanck, F. and Grynberg, M. (2010). "Prejudice, transgenerational transmission, and neutrality". *International Journal of Psycho-analysis*, 91, 1216–1219.

Faimberg, H. (1993). *"La Transmisión de la vida psíquica entre generaciones"* (The transmission of psychic life between generations). Amorrortu, Buenos Aires.

Freud, S (1878). "The Project." In *Collected Works*, Vol. 1. Amorrortu, Buenos Aires.

Freud, S. (1916–17). "Lecture 18. The fixation to trauma. The Unconscious." In *Collected Works*. Amorrortu, Buenos Aires.

Freud, S. (1919). "The Uncanny". In *Collected Works*, Vol. XVII. Amorrortu, Buenos Aires.

Moliner, M. (2007). *Diccionario de uso del Español*. Editorial Gredos, SAU, Madrid.

Viñar, M. (2003). "El reconocimiento del prójimo. Notas para pensar el otro extranjero" (The recognition of the other. Notes for thinking about the foreign other). In *El otro, el extranjero*, pp. 35–48. Zorzal, Buenos Aires.

Viñar, M. (2008). "Derechos Humanos y el Psicoanálisis" (Human Rights and Psychoanalysis). *Revista Uruguaya de Psicoanálisis*, 106, 149–174.

Volnovich, J.C. (2003). "Contratransferencia a lo largo de la historia" (Counter-transference throughout history). See www.topia.com.ar/artículos/39cl-volnovich.htm

Woscoboinik, J. (2000). "La razón de la sinrazón" (The reason of unreason). *Revista de psicoanálisis*, 57, 4, pp. 341–357.

Chapter 6

The Logic of Prejudice

Ulises Schmill

In order to find an orientation—not always correct—about the meaning of some phenomenon, it is convenient first to turn to a dictionary to check the way in which the word referring to it has been understood. Therefore, as a first approximation, the *Diccionario del Español Actual* by Manuel Seco, Olimpia Andrés and Gabino Ramos explains the use of the word "prejudice" as follows: (a) "a preconceived belief or opinion" and (b) "a recurring idea about behaviour imposed by education or the environment". To fully understand this concept, it is necessary to know what is meant by "preconception": "to conceive beforehand (an idea or a feeling)".

These definitions do not allow us to reach a complete understanding of prejudice. However, they point to certain facts that can be used to understand what the phenomenon of prejudice is and how it operates in everyday life. We must start from human behaviour and determine the causes and conditions of its emergence. For this, there is no better author to refer to than the behavioural psychologist B.F. Skinner and his concept of operant behaviour.[1] Behaviour can be conceived as a series of specific movements of the human (or animal) body that produces (operates or generates) specific consequences in the environment, one of which may be a positive reinforcer (pleasure or well-being), in the sense that it increases the probability of repetition of the behaviour, or it may produce aversive consequences (unpleasant or painful) that will increase the probability of omitting the behaviour. In the latter case, the behaviour is punished with those consequences. Just think of the firing of a gun. The bodily movement consists of the flexing of a finger on the trigger of a gun, which triggers a series of chemical, mechanical and biological processes that lead to the death of a certain person. All these external processes are the causal consequences of a person's behaviour of flexing the index finger of his or her right hand on the trigger of a gun. Generalising, we could say that all behaviour generates consequences.

However, certain types of behaviour, in specific environments or settings, produce consequences on a regular basis, without exception. Whoever performs the bodily movement in the circumstances described can be sure that consequences will occur, consequences that may be of a natural or predominantly social

DOI: 10.4324/9781003291978-7

character (in this case, think of the child who is punished, without exception, when he or she tells a lie, in an authoritarian family environment, as might well be described). The latter would be the case with respect to a very strict social environment. In other cases, consequences are random; they may occur or sometimes fail to occur, especially if they are social in nature, as rewards and punishments do not occur by causal necessity, but are given or imposed by human beings on the occasion of behaviours performed by other individuals. As all behaviour is carried out because of the consequences it produces (Skinnerian operant behaviour), which are unfailing or random, in the two circumstances mentioned above there is a proclivity and probability that prescriptive rules (orders, commands) of different content will be formulated in each case considered.

One, when the consequences are unfailing, the prescription (the order or command issued) may be imperative, specifying exclusively the conduct it is intended to motivate, disregarding the consequences and emphasising exclusively the inner character or internal disposition of the subject and the conviction with which he or she executes the rule, disregarding any external circumstance as irrelevant, as the desired consequences will always and regularly occur. Mention of these consequences can be omitted. Kant is perhaps the most conspicuous example of this tendency. Let us not forget that he grew up in an atmosphere of deep pietistic religiosity, with its emphasis on the inner aspects of conduct and morality. He says:

> A good will is good not because of what it performs or effects, not by its aptness for the attainment of some proposed end, but simply by virtue of the volition; that is, it is good in itself, and considered by itself is to be esteemed much higher than all that can be brought about by it in favour of any inclination, nay even of the sum total of all inclinations. Even if it should happen that, owing to special disfavour of fortune, or the niggardly provision of a step-motherly nature, this will should wholly lack power to accomplish its purpose, if with its greatest efforts it should yet achieve nothing, and there should remain only the good will (not, to be sure, a mere wish, but the summoning of all means in our power), then, like a jewel, it would still shine by its own light, as a thing which has its whole value in itself. Its usefulness or fruitlessness can neither add nor take away anything from this value.[2]

Two, when the consequences are random, the prescription must be formulated conditionally and point out, in all neatness, those consequences. In this case, there is a tendency to disregard the internal aspects of the subject, his or her strength of character and conviction to carry out the conduct. This, in itself, is meaningless to the prescriber. Only the result, however it is achieved, is of interest. The prescriptions have a markedly objectivist tendency, prone to utilitarianism. "The road to hell is paved with good intentions", according to a popular saying, which is absolutely in line with the ethics of responsibility as described by Max Weber.[3] According to this view, it is not possible to disregard the consequences and results of one's own conduct, because pure intention is not a sufficient guarantee that the consequent conduct will not lead to a situation that could legitimately be described as hellish.

In the concept of prejudice provided by the above-mentioned dictionary, it is stated that prejudice is a belief or opinion, imposed by education or the environment, that functions as a conceptual or emotive ground for a behaviour. As we have already had the opportunity to say, the meaning of the reinforcement contingency (behaviour + consequences) can be formulated with maxims or statements that mention the consequences of the behaviour. Specific emotions or feelings—pleasant or agreeable in the case of a positive reinforcement or aversive and unpleasant in the case of an unfavourable consequence—can and are associated with the meanings of the behaviour. In this way, learning processes are installed that will condition and determine future behaviours when the subject is faced with situations similar to those that generated those learning processes.

The problem of prejudice arises when behaviour in the present is motivated by a specific idea or belief or, more importantly, by a correlative emotion towards a certain object or situation and is reacted to on the basis of that previously generated belief or idea or driven by feelings arising from discriminative stimuli similar or identical to those that generated the ideas or emotions that are operating in the present.

The concept of prejudice arises from the comparison between the ideas or beliefs that motivate a conduct or a judgement in the present, before a determined object or situation, conduct or judgement that, from a certain objective point of view, does not agree with the characteristic notes of the real situation and that would determine a conduct or judgement radically different from the one that would be rationally pertinent. That is to say, the meaning of a conduct with its consequences learned in the past operates in the present reality, without into account the characteristic notes of the present situation or object, which would be the rationally pertinent one. This is the essential point.

If someone has acquired, through education, the belief that human beings of colour in the United States only like jazz music, he or she will react favourably or unfavourably to a human being of colour or accept or reject a judgement about them, based on that belief, without objectively considering that there are musicians of colour who are great symphonic music artists such as James DePreist (conductor) or André Watts (pianist). This is a very elementary example without serious consequences. But there are prejudices that can lead to behaviour that is truly harmful to other human beings, all of them based on prejudices acquired in earlier stages of learning development. Constellations of prejudice of this kind are, in general, all religions, which inculcate certain conceptions in the consciousness of believers that will determine their future behaviour towards themselves or their fellow human beings, or policies such as those held and carried out by Hitler's National Socialism or the behaviour of the Bolshevik Stalin.

What is the fundamental logical characteristic of behaviour generated by prejudice? To find it, it is first necessary to formulate the statements that describe the behaviour and the content of the prejudice, for it is only in relation to these statements that we can characterise the logical structure of how the prejudice operates. If an American character says that an Arab-looking person is a terrorist, he or she is judging on the basis of a prejudice, because, without investigating his or her background and biography, education and experiences, the statement "X is a terrorist" is not justified. On the basis of this conception, he or she may act immediately by distancing him- or herself from the person or rejecting any attempt at fraternisation, as well as engaging in a number of other specific behaviours that may be a consequence of his or her prejudice. Thus, we have formulated the content of the prejudice and the statement describing one of the consequences of the prejudice. Generally, the subject acting on the basis of a prejudice has the capacity to formulate the content of the prejudice and to make it explicit. But this is not always the case. We have already observed that, in many cases, the consequences learned in reinforcement contingencies (or learning processes) are accompanied by emotions and feelings that predominantly appear before the content of the prejudice can be made clear. Feelings and emotions are immediate triggers of behaviour and become the most powerful motivating element.

Given the above, in one or other form of conditioning behaviour, the content of the prejudice or the sense of the feeling that accompanies it is generally not explicitly expressed, and it happens that the subject acts apparently in a mysterious way, as he or she has not formulated all the implicit premises of his or her behaviour. The description of the latter then becomes a logical structure called an *enthymeme*, which is the logical figure of a deduction in which one or more premises have been omitted. To express it in the words of J. Ferrater Mora:

> the enthymeme is an incomplete syllogism, because one of the premises is not expressed. If the major premise is missing, the enthymeme is called of the first order; if the minor premise is missing, it is called of the second order. Thus, "Bulgarians drink kefir; Bulgarians are in good health" is an enthymeme of the first order. "All Englishmen read novels; John Smith reads novels" is a second-order enthymeme.[4]

In the first example, the major premise, "All those who drink kefir are in good health", is missing; in the second example, the minor premise, "John Smith is apparently English", has been omitted. The possibility of a chaining of multiple enthymemes in such a way that one functions as a link to the next should not be surprising. This may become apparent if the corresponding syllogisms are completed, and the omitted premises are formulated in their entirety—that is, if the enthymematic syllogism is defeated; for example,

"Bulgarians do not visit the doctor often", "Bulgarians take little medicine" and so on. It is an enthymematic chain: p^1, p^2, p^3 and so on.

In relation to this topic, it is useful to consider Paul Grice's theory of implicatures, which can be considered a theory that makes explicit the rules that, in face-to-face communications, speakers use to understand more of what is said and that can be considered a method for identifying speakers' biases—that is, for determining the premises omitted in the verbal exchange. Many verbal exchanges are carried out with great ease because the listener follows the rules derived from Grice's principle of cooperation and those of the author's principle of opposition. I want to be more explicit.

Paul Grice's Implications: The Principle of Cooperation[5]

The English philosopher Paul Grice's theory of implicatures attempts to explain how it is possible to mean more with an utterance or a verbal expression than what is literally said in it. Purely semantic analysis of words will not provide the totality of the information they convey, information that can be determined as the premises omitted in the enthymeme where a pre-judice operates. All that we can reasonably expect semantic theory to tell us about some verbal exchange can be exemplified as follows:

O1: Can you tell me the time?
O2: (pragmatically interpreted particle) The milkman has already left.

It is clear to speakers of the language that what is communicated in such an exchange is greater than what is explicitly said verbally. This additional meaning is recorded in the following possible verbal exchange, where the listener's understanding is made explicit:

O1: Could you tell me what time it is at the moment, as shown in the standard way by your wristwatch, and would you be so kind as to tell me?
O2: No, I don't know what the exact time is at the moment, but I can give you some information from which *you can deduce the approximate time*, namely: the milkman has already left.[6]

Everything written in italics is part of what was communicated in the verbal exchange, but it is noticeable that not everything that was communicated was *said*. How is this possible?

Grice's proposal is that there is a set of assumptions or rules that guide and determine verbal behaviour in conversation. Levinson says: "These [assumptions or rules], it seems, arise from basic rational considerations and can be formulated as master guides for the effective and efficient use of language in conversation for further cooperative purposes."[7]

These assumptions guiding and determining verbal behaviour can be formulated into a set of rules or maxims of verbal behaviour in conversation and a general cooperative principle encompassing and comprising them. Levinson formulates them as follows:

- *Cooperative principle*: make your contribution as it is required, at the stage at which it occurs for the accepted purpose or in the direction of the verbal exchange in which you find yourself.
- *Quality maxim*: make your contribution true; specifically: (a) do not say what you believe to be false; (b) do not say what you lack adequate evidence for.
- *Maxim of quantity*: (a) make your contribution as informative as is required for the current purposes of the exchange; (b) do not make your contribution more informative than is required.
- *Maxim of relevance*: make your contribution relevant.
- *Maxim of manner*: be insightful and especially: (a) avoid obscurities; (b) avoid ambiguities; (c) be brief; (d) be tidy.

Grice's thesis asserts that the cooperative principle and maxims effectively guide the behaviour of the subjects involved in the verbal exchange. When there is an apparent superficial violation of them, the participants interpret what happened in accordance with them, making the necessary inferences that allow them to interpret the exchange as a regular instance—that is, an instance in which the maxims and the principle have been complied with.

Rather, in the most common kinds of conversations these principles guide them, so that when conversations appear not to be in accordance with their specifications, listeners assume that, contrary to appearances, however, the principles are still operating at a deeper level.[8]

The Principle of Opposition and Its Maxims

Following the same Gricean scheme, to make the comparison easier, let us formulate the principle of opposition and its maxims:

- *Principle of opposition or belligerence*: do not make your contribution as required by the speaker, favouring his interests, either at the stage at which it should occur, or with the object of benefiting the verbal exchange in which you find yourself, although you must maintain the appearance of cooperating.
- *Maxim of quality*: the contribution need not be true: (a) say what is false; (b) say what you do not have adequate evidence for.
- *Maxim of quantity*: (a) do not give all the information; (b) give too much information.

- *Maxim of relevance*: present information riddled with irrelevant elements.
- *Maxim of manner*: do not be perspicuous: (a) produce obscurities; (b) produce ambiguities; (c) be neat; (d) be messy.

With the principle of opposition or belligerence, it is possible to explain those cases in which something is understood contrary to what has been expressly said or manifested. In fact, suspicion is the customary exercise of this principle. Where "yes" is said, "no" is understood; if "never x" is stated, "always x" is understood and vice versa; probability is certainty, and the apodictic is merely plausible; the necessary is transmuted into the impossible; and what is not plausible is believed with absolute conviction. The principle of opposition is the perfect counterpart of the cooperative principle. This is understandable, as prima facie both arise from situations that are opposite in their characteristics: plurality of complementary values on non-scarce goods and identity of valuations on scarce goods.

Elements of Verbal Exchange

In every verbal exchange, there are two subjects who participate with their linguistic utterances, which we can call the speaker and the hearer. Each, in the course of a verbal exchange, changes roles, the speaker becoming the listener at a later point in time and vice versa.

If we consider the two principles and their maxims that we have outlined, it is possible to construct conceptually a combination in the efficiency of these principles in the hearer or in the speaker. It may happen that, in the verbal exchange, both are applying the principle of cooperation, in a position that can be described as symmetrical. Listener and speaker cooperate with each other. But it may happen that the situation is not symmetrical, so that one applies one principle while the other applies the other principle. This is implicit in the formulation of the principle of opposition: if you want to succeed, you must pretend to cooperate. The principle of opposition is the maxim of all deceitful, lying, untruthful behaviour. It is the maxim applied by all those who want to take advantage of their fellow human beings, who want to exploit them or benefit from them. Weber points out in his book *Economy and Society* that, between rulers and subjects, there is inevitably opposition and struggle. Therefore, we are presented with the following combinatory possibilities of what we are talking about: listener and speaker apply the principle of cooperation; they are in symmetrical positions. The speaker applies the principle of opposition, and the listener applies the principle of cooperation or, conversely, the listener applies the principle of opposition, and the speaker applies the principle of cooperation. These two situations are what generate irreconcilable disagreements and mis-understandings, which are so common in family and, especially, marital relationships. In the political sphere, all the possibilities of asymmetry are present, as ideologies can be understood as the application of the principle

of opposition by the ruler in order to obtain compliance with his orders and
mandates by the subjects or those subject to his empire. Max Weber's principles of legitimacy are examples of such ideologies. To illustrate the above,
let me give the following example:

A paradigmatic example can be found in the roles played by the two main
characters in the tragedy of *Othello*. Iago acts according to the principle of
opposition or belligerence, while Othello acts under the principle of cooperation,
considering the words of his enemy as manifestations of the "honest Iago" who
wants to communicate true information to him with his brief insinuations, to
which Othello applies the rules of the principle of cooperation and obtains the
disastrous conclusions that lead him to murder his fair wife. But, in the very
interesting verbal exchanges between the two characters, the final one reveals the
underlying prejudice of the Venetian general. Read Act III, Scene 3 carefully, to
realise what I have said. What is the prejudice that overwhelms Othello, which is
brutally revealed to him in the words of Iago? Says this character:

IAGO: I know our country disposition well;
    In Venice they do let heaven see the pranks
    They dare not show their husbands; their best conscience
    Is not to leave't undone, but keep't unknown. [...]
    She did deceive her father, marrying you;
    And when she seem'd to shake and fear your looks,
    She loved them most. [...]
    Why, go to then;
    She that, so young, could give out such a seeming,
    To seal her father's eyes up close as oak—
    He thought 'twas witchcraft—but I am much to blame;
    I humbly do beseech you of your pardon
    For too much loving you.[9]

Then Othello hears from Iago's lips the prejudice he did not know and
would not have dared to formulate and express:

    Ay, there's the point: as—to be bold with you—
    Not to affect many proposed matches
    Of her own clime, complexion, and degree,
    Whereto we see in all things nature tends—
    Foh! one may smell in such a will most rank,
    Foul disproportion thoughts unnatural.
    But pardon me; I do not in position
    Distinctly speak of her; though I may fear
    Her will, recoiling to her better judgment,
    May fall to match you with her country forms
    And happily repent.

Evil rose to his feet so that he could walk and carry out his murderous deed. It follows that the Moor, general of Venice, married to the fair Desdemona, is prey to a prejudice that he had never formulated and of which he was unaware until the moment when the cunning words of his enemy made it known to him. Othello falls into the nets of his own prejudice: as a black man, he cannot trust the white inhabitants of Venice, and even less the perverse false women, one of whom, the most beautiful, has preferred him, despite his colour, to the Venetian suitors, also white and perhaps blond. The racist prejudice that he did not know determined him is the one that appears in Iago's words. He acknowledges it when he says: "This fellow's of exceeding honesty, and knows all qualities, with a learned spirit, of human dealings".

With the above, I wanted to show the reader that Grice's thesis and my thesis of the principle of opposition are methods that can help to discover the prejudices that operate in the conscience of the human being or in his or her feelings and that constitute all qualities "of human dealings", as Othello puts it.

In summary, in this chapter, I have tried to expose some learning processes, based on Skinner's behaviourist theory, and how experienced reinforcement contingencies can give rise to the formation of biases. I have explicitly provided a concept of prejudice and stated that prejudices can be explained in their logical functioning as enthymemes—that is, the meaning of the actual behaviour is not made explicit by stating all its premises, thus constituting the logical figure of the enthymeme. I then related this logical peculiarity of prejudice to Paul Grice's theory of implicatures and their rules and have ended by exemplifying this with Shakespeare's tragedy of *Othello*.

Notes

1 We stick to a simple behaviourist stance in order not to get into psychological (mentalistic) or cognitive problems, which are not essential for our purposes.
2 Translated from the German text, *Fundamentación de la metafísica de las costumbres* (1785), by Thomas Kingsmill Abbott.
3 Max Weber, 1921.
4 José Ferrater Mora, 2001, p. 1030.
5 Ulises Schmill, 2010.
6 Stephen C. Levinson, 1983, p. 98.
7 Ibid., p. 101.
8 Ibid., p. 102.
9 William Shakespeare, *Othello, The Moor of Venice*. Act III, Scene 3.

References

Ferrater Mora, José, *Diccionario de Filosofía*, Vol. II. Barcelona, Ariel, 2001.
Levinson, Stephen C., *Pragmatics*. Cambridge, Cambridge University Press, 1983.

Schmill, Ulises, *Las Implicaturas del Resentimiento. La Tragedia de Otelo* (The Tragedy of Othello). México, Themis, 2010.
Shakespeare, William, *Othello, The Moor of Venice.* Act III, Scene 3.
Weber, Max, *Politics as a Vocation.* Originally published as *Politik als Beruf, Gesammelte Politische Schriften.* Munich, 1921.

Chapter 7

Biological Roots of Prejudice

Marcelino Cereijido

I think I realise that the concept of "prejudice" is a kind of projective test, which brings to light the ills that those who try to define it attribute to the "other". To begin at home, I am sure that my views on prejudice come to identify and perhaps single me out, because so far there are not many who share them, but neither am I oblivious to the frustrated exasperation of those who try to refute me. Let us consider my discomfort with what we might call "the orthodox version" of prejudice: (a) Traditionally and formally, "prejudice" is taken as if it were a fundamentally ethical problem; however, ethics is a branch of philosophy that studies morality consciously and rationally, whereas, for me, the most powerful components of prejudice have little to do with consciousness and almost nothing to do with reason. (b) When something is unique to a particular society or era, such as a language, a form of government, a school of painting, it is considered to be a product of culture, but, when it is observed in all people, all peoples on Earth and throughout history and even prehistory, such as coughing, sleeping, jealousy, laughing, crying, it is suspected that it must have biological roots, in which case, to understand why humans have these attributes, it is essential to trace their biological evolution. I am not saying that today we have the same prejudices that the Chaldeans had, but I am saying that they had prejudices, which served essentially the same functions as they do among us in the 21st century. (c) However, until a few decades ago, anyone who suggested the possibility that any human attribute with a cultural impact, such as being prejudiced, might have biological roots was silenced and vilified in order to chastise and dissuade anyone who doubted that everything must be played out at the level of ethics. (d) As I will argue in due course, prejudice has strong biological and also supra-personal components, in the sense that, in addition to his or her own prejudices, a person reflects those of his or her group(s) of belonging.

Natural Selection Is Essential

Theodosius Dobzhansky made a recommendation so convincing that it has become a catchphrase: "In biology nothing makes sense outside the context

DOI: 10.4324/9781003291978-8

of evolution". He meant that, if we want to understand why a toucan has such an exaggerated beak, a mole is almost blind or we see a reality in colour, it is essential to review the phylogeny of the trait and the species in question. Because, as I mentioned in the previous paragraph, prejudice has strong biological components, it is useful to refresh some evolutionary concepts that might be involved: (a) The survival of organisms depends on their ability to interpret their reality effectively. A slug, such a simple creature that does not even have a brain, needs to be able to detect whether nutrients have run out to its left but there are still nutrients to its right and to move in that direction. Similarly, if in a field with thousands of sunflowers we were to detect a sunflower with its corolla facing away from the sun, we would know that it is misinterpreting reality, and its chance of leaving fertile sunflower offspring is almost nil. Natural selection is thus purifying the species until, after millions of years of testing them, today slugs and sunflowers satisfactorily interpret the reality that concerns them. (b) As far as we know, a slug and a sunflower do not have consciousness, and so the interpretation they make of reality is unconscious. (c) All species develop some quality that becomes their *tool and weapon* for the struggle for life. (d) This tool-and-weapon is continually perfected by natural selection, which favours the survival of species that have *complementary attributes* to that main tool-and-weapon.

Let us think of a giraffe that can eat leaves from the treetops without climbing them because evolution has selected from among its ancestors those with long legs and neck, but, *complementarily*, it has also selected giraffes with a huge heart (about 6 kilograms), capable of pumping blood and irrigating a brain located 2 metres higher; otherwise, the giraffe would faint and die. However, this was not enough to make giraffes viable, and so giraffes with more complementary attributes were selected, otherwise the blood pressure that the heart needs to pump blood to reach the brain when the animal's neck is upright would cause it to burst when it lowered its head to drink water from a pond 6 metres below. In short, only those giraffes have survived (have been selected) that, in *addition to* being 5 or 6 metres tall and having a powerful heart, have developed a system of valves in the lumen of their vessels that protect them against excess blood pressure when they lower their heads to the level of their hooves. It is because of the sum of these details that we could then say with a certain humorous touch that no animal surpasses the giraffe in being a giraffe.

The Evolution of *Homo sapiens*

Homo sapiens are no exception; both our structures and our ways of functioning were built and assembled by unconscious mechanisms, and, furthermore, our way of interpreting reality is dominated by unconscious mechanisms. Let us look at some of them: (a) The cells of our intestinal mucosa absorb the iron contained in our diet, which the organism uses in the synthesis of haemoglobin. We would die hopelessly if the interpretation that iron is that element that wanders in the half-digested pasta that arrives from the stomach after eating spinach or pork chops were to fail. At the moment, we, consciously, with our modern science, have just begun to interpret it over the last half-century, but it is obvious that cells have been doing it for millions of years. All the great essential achievements that make life function and structure life on the planet were then products of unconscious mechanisms that continue to be unconscious today. Consciousness is a newcomer to the stage of life, because life originated some 4.5 billion years ago – and has been evolving since – while consciousness is barely 50,000 years old (that is, 0.00005 million, some 80,000 times more recent). Suffice it to say that, by the time something we can call consciousness arose, the great dinosaurs were already extinct, there were already birds and flowers in the four corners of the planet, and our species, *Homo sapiens*, had been wandering around like a kind of autistic in a Stone Age that was almost at its end. (c) The construction of our brain and the mind that emerges from it as one more of its many emergent functions are, therefore, products of a completely unconscious biological functioning. No one knows how our mother built our brain, or how we maintain and repair it. But they did it; what counts for life is that what is carried out arises from a correct interpretation of reality, and it matters very little whether or not the organism is conscious of interpreting it, for it is as relevant as asking whether or not a computer running an oil refinery is conscious of the task it is carrying out: it is enough that it manages to make it work efficiently, and that is it.

Nowadays, when we mention the "unconscious", it is essential to clarify that we are only referring to a functioning independent of our consciousness, and therefore different from the "unconscious" that psychoanalysts study, which is the product of a complex interaction of the subject with his or her parents and with culture and has different levels of accessibility, interdictions and taboos, but to which I will *not* allude in the present chapter.

It is obvious that the human tool-and-weapon to fight for life arises from a tremendous hypertrophy of our capacity to interpret reality, but, as in previous paragraphs, we have assigned so much importance to complementary attributes, it is worth looking at some that have been co-selected in the case of *Homo sapiens* and that may foreseeably play a role in prejudice. (a) Thus, a huge and heterogeneous *memory* has been selected, which stores not only data (names, quantities, places), but also aromas, tastes, colours, voices. And here, again, we are not aware of where in the brain the neuronal circuits and encephalic centres are that transport and store the information captured by the tactile, auditory and olfactory pathways, or of how they are recorded or, as neurobiologists say, in which neuron and in which molecular structures we have stored the image of our grandmother that allows us to recognise her in a photograph. (b) The capacity to merge the contents of the various memories in such a way that we evoke a *unified image* of reality has also been selected, a capacity that is mysterious for the moment, given that the information provided by each sense, perhaps contained in memories stored in different parts of the brain, does not seem easily to merge with that provided by the others: red does not smell, salty does not sound, the touch that reveals that something is rough/smooth has nothing to do with whether it is sweet or sour. (c) We *Homo sapiens* have also been selected for our *sense of time*, which leads us to admit that there is a *time*, which we cannot even convincingly define, let alone prove that it exists, but which allows us to make dynamic models of reality (i.e. in terms of that time). (d) It is obvious that we have also been selected for being *believers*. Thanks to this property, we not only incorporate into our cognitive heritage everything we have discovered and found out for ourselves, but also what other human beings on the planet, from generations before us, have learned. I, for example, did not personally know Tutankhamun, nor did I discover the atomic nucleus, nor did I invent Spanish, but I have incorporated them into my cognitive heritage thanks to the fact that I "believed" them from my parents, teachers and society, through upbringing, formal education and coexistence. To make matters worse, most of these things, especially the most fundamental ones, were incorporated when I did not yet have the capacity to reason in order to filter and exclude inanities and perversities. (e) The unconscious can manage very well on its own, without the assistance of consciousness, as all non-biological organisms lack a consciousness (at least one identical to ours), and the unconscious is in charge of life 24 hours a day. (f) That unconscious, acting on its own, was enough for species to develop and give rise to a fabulous biological diversity over billions of years. Consciousness has a very restricted working schedule, as it takes hours of rest at night, while the unconscious is still there, in charge of biology. It also attends to the lion's body even during the 20 hours a day that it sleeps, and the 24 hours that a polar bear sleeps when it hibernates for 4 months. (g) Furthermore, where do we get the idea that, when consciousness emerged, it took the form of an enveloping and impermeable capsule, a sort of iron curtain whose key was placed in the hands of the consciousness and which chose to cancel all direct communication between the unconscious and the surrounding reality? It is like taking it for granted that, because a person has bought a spyglass, he will henceforth be obliged not to look at reality directly, but will read books through the spyglass, shave while looking at himself in the mirror through the spyglass, make love while looking at his or her partner through the spyglass. It seems that it must be the other way around: the unconscious continues to be in charge of our exchange with the environment and other organisms (including, of course, those of the family and human society), as it has been doing for billions of years, and only decides to make use of consciousness in special cases. Finally, if prejudice were a conscious matter, one would have to admit something as untenable as that primitive men, those who existed thousands of years ago, before the emergence of consciousness, could not have been prejudiced.[1]

Patterns and Senses

Information can be stored in a library, in a computer memory and in many other ways; *knowledge*, on the other hand, needs the mind that knows, but we still do not know how the mind transforms information into knowledge. And, in this vein, we also do not know how it makes *sense* of life. Since the dawn of history, human beings seem to have relied on a quality control of their perceptions and knowledge called *"sense"*. As long as humans saw the cat walking by and the pigeon flying by, everything was fine, and they did not even notice it. But, if they suddenly saw the cat flying by, that required all the attention they could summon! A Christian was indoctrinated to believe that the meaning of his or her life was to be passing through the world long enough for God to observe how he or she behaved and, consequently, to send him or her to paradise or hell. The power of meaning is incredibly powerful and effective. When I was a medical student, I was amazed to observe terminally ill cancer patients, desperate as soon as it became clear to them that they were in agony, who were soothed by the visit of a confessing priest who reminded them that we are passing through the world; moreover, from then on, it was likely that they themselves would be the ones to soothe their grieving bereaved. These cognitive placebos, amalgamated into something we called "the meaning of life", had the virtue of soothing human pain. It was enough that the message came disguised as an explanation: "as fate would have it", "we are nothing". If there was an explanation, even if you didn't understand it, it made sense, and, if it made sense, everything was fine, and you need not bother to analyse arguments, if you knew how to do so.

A very similar phenomenon, but on a smaller scale, concerns the *patterns* that govern our unconscious behaviours. Perhaps they are signs, tracks or clues that an animal or a person groups together, without knowing why and perhaps without consciously realising that they are grouping them together, but that are enough for our unconscious to lead us to affirm, "this is my mother's face", without any doubt or need for demonstration. Of course, in other contexts, the patterns trigger highly complex neuroendocrine mechanisms that never pass through our consciousness. For example, the slightly asymmetrical face of a person or animal is used by prospective spouses as a clue that the genetic endowment of their prospective spouse is not sufficiently tuned and leads him or her to desist from sexual intercourse. If we accept that dogs, cats and rats do not have consciousness, we can say that these cues to pick up on whether our prospective spouse is processing their genes properly work unconsciously. But the issue must be much more complex and deeper, because dogs, cats, and rats do not know about genes, and, before Gregor Mendel, we humans did not know either. And so, there are people who desist from an action because they come across a black cat, hotels that do not have rooms on the 13th floor listed because clients prefer not to stay in them, people who continue to repel the left-handed as sinister, and others who, if one mentions a certain risk in some action they are going to undertake, instead of being grateful for the advice and taking precautions, take it as a summons to the deities of evil. "*Don't throw salt on me*", they often exclaim with hostility. It is not even essential for life that the prejudices implied in these patterns are transformed into explanations that can be collated into arguments, let alone explanations. There is the famous response of trumpeter Louis Armstrong to someone who asked him what jazz is: "Man! If you need to ask, you'll never understand".

Finally, something is more easily believed when it matches what is expected or desired, even if it is a falsehood. Who could have convinced Christopher Columbus that the continent he had just found was not India! It fitted his desires and expectations. The impression that the discovery left on his European contemporaries was so remarkable that no one could erase the term "Indians" from the natives of the Americas. In his book *The Believing Brain*, Michael Shermer lists 25 prejudices that bog down *reason* to the point where it accepts pseudo-scientific conclusions.[2] This shows that reason can assemble its arguments in a certain way that *pleases* the unconscious. And there we have the *placebo* in full swing. Shermer calls the tendency to search for, find and reinterpret confirmatory evidence "the mother of all prejudices and biases".[3] With all that, the brain manufactures a *heuristic* – a method for solving problems through intuition, trial and error – or any other method, however informal, that matches what we want to prove. Hence the famous saying "There is no one in this world stupid enough not to be able to find facts to support their point of view". The brain certainly knows how to reason, but it often refuses to do so. It knows that the size of a shoe depends in a complex way on age, height, weight, sex, model and a thousand other variables, but it chooses to try one on and, based on that experience, ask for a bigger or smaller or taller shoe and prefers that the shoemaker does not show it anthropological tables and nomograms about the relationship between shoe size and each one of them or fill in a long questionnaire that a computer could adjust with an equation to suggest the right size. Luckily, we are not the *Homo rationalis* we once imagined – and discarded; we are *Homo sapiens* and *we* know that everything is easier by trying on one or two sizes.

Attributes That Are Gradually Installed in Each New Human Being

As the child progresses towards adulthood, she comes to see for herself, in her own confrontation with reality, what she had been believing her parents and teachers to believe. However, there are many beliefs, specific to the culture in which the child was born, that are only validated by faith – that is to say, they are not validated by testing reality, as happens with "fire burns", "the knife cuts", "honey is sweet", but because other members of the community continue to impart teachings to the child that reinforce what her parents had instilled in her. But, as neurobiologist José M. Musacchio points out,[4] faith is riddled with misunderstandings, because it is about explanations that were coined before there was any way to be certain, and it does not serve to discriminate between false and true beliefs.

> Based on the mix of beliefs that families choose to raise their child with, an individual can be programmed from early childhood to become anything imaginable, from a Tibetan monk to a kamikaze pilot, as long as the right imprints are ingrained in them.[5]

These imprints are usually made at such an early age that the child does not yet have the capacity to reasonably assess what is being imprinted on her.

The popular belief prevails that the child lives in a world of wild fantasies (as she usually tells them herself) and can be brought up on the basis of toy ideas, wooden horses, tin trains and white lies, but, one day, like a snake that suddenly sheds its skin en bloc or a spider that in its growing stages will shed its exoskeleton as if it were a shell, she will remove these crusts of fantasies and come to her senses. The matter must be more complicated, as an adult who has been indoctrinated with hoaxes in childhood resorts to making them acceptable by renaming them "tradition" and comes to accept some others as "white lies" so as not to frustrate his elders. How can he give grandparents a hard time by not marrying in a religious ceremony or refusing to baptise their great-grandchild?

Music and painting provide everyday examples of how a belief that neither we nor our parents may have held can be rationally eliminated *as a true fact* but can still influence our lives, even if it is now mere myth and hoax, for most of us who are delighted and moved by Mozart's, Brahms's and Verdi's *Requiems*, Bach's *The Passion According to St Matthew* and *The Passion According to St John*, Dvořák's or Penderecki's *Stabat Mater*, the stained-glass windows of Chartres, the Sistine Chapel or Michelangelo's *Pietà*, do not believe at all what they narrate or represent. In other words, beliefs, even if they are not our own, become prejudices, whose roots are much deeper and more dominant than the rational positions of ethics.

The Prejudiced Person Does Not Test His or Her Prejudices: She or He Hoards Them

On a visit to the United Nations, the prime minister of a certain country refused to shake hands with Secretary-General Kofi Annan, who was receiving him as a matter of protocol. The foreign minister of that country tried to apologise, but he was evidently no less majestic than his fellow countryman: "In my country, we think that when we shake hands with a black man, we get a dirty hand". Does the reader honestly believe that everything would have been solved by bringing some Petri dishes with gels and broths and asking Kofi Annan and the prime minister to dip their hands in them to analyse what contaminants and species of micro-organisms they carried? If the reader thought so, he or she would disagree with the vast majority of newspaper readers who consider this to be outrageous prejudice. Cesare Cremonini, a professor in Padua, refused to look through his colleague Galileo Galilei's brand-new telescope to see with his own eyes that Jupiter is indeed orbited by four moons. To review one last example: Catholics believe that, during the Eucharist, the host and wine that the priest consecrates are transubstantiated into the body and blood of Jesus. It would be extremely easy to settle the matter by taking a few millilitres of the liquid from the chalice to find out to which blood group Jesus belonged, and, as blood contains white blood cells with DNA in their nucleus, its genome could be sequenced in passing, which would yield valuable information about the genes of Mary, the Holy Spirit and even the Judeo-Christian god. We see from these examples that the prejudiced person *prefers to safeguard his or her prejudice* to avoid a confrontation with reality, which is one of the coarsest forms of lying.

1   *Stubbornness*: The mathematician and philosopher Alfred North Whitehead was of the opinion that a concept becomes dogma the moment it is disputed. But, as we saw in the previous paragraph, the prejudiced person never willingly offers to test his or her assertions, so he or she always defends dogmas, even if what he or she asserts is provable.[6] On the contrary, he or she protects the crucial aspects of his or her position with a suspicion bordering on the paranoid. This stubbornness is an aberration, because it is nothing more than the red-hot principle of authority. By this principle, something is true or false depending on who says it: the Bible, the Pope, the king, the father. The prejudiced person expects, with foolish honesty, that the fact that he or she, his or her institution and his or her people enunciate and endorse a certain conception[7] should suffice as proof that it is true.[8]

2   The prejudiced person claims the *right* to hold prejudiced ideas (which, I repeat, she or he continues to take as truthful alternatives).[9] There is nothing *judgemental* about pre-judgement; it is a vulgar attempt to claim the right to lie, which, today, those who grant it propose to euphemistically call "tolerance".

3   Prejudiced people *come to establish tacit non-aggression pacts*: if they suddenly detect that their interlocutor also has objectionable grounds of argument, only of a different sign, they may begin to move towards a bilateral pact that gives their prejudices the value of bargaining chips.

4   It is suspicious that, over the years, the prejudiced find and collect arguments that always favour their cause and rarely come across any that weaken or refute it; if they were to come across a refutation, it would not be strategically convenient for them to declare it.

5   Both the victors and the vanquished generate *official histories* that are, to put it in black and white, hagiographies that treasure positive evidence,

while softening, excusing and forgetting the negative. The victim also claims the heritage of *his or her* "official" version and does not allow anyone to suggest a different explanation. It is in bad taste to make the slightest objection to an exile or someone who was tortured.

The question then arises: what *good are* prejudices to the prejudiced person, enough to hold on to them so jealously and indulge in fallacious rituals to defend them?

It Is Impossible Not to Be Prejudiced

To begin with: we cannot start from a sound core of reasoning because we do *not have a cognitive heritage resistant to falsehoods*. Even mathematical knowledge itself must start from *axioms*. The word "axiom" comes from the Greek noun αξιωμα, meaning "that which *seems* right" or *is considered* self-evident, without the need for demonstration. Worse is the case of *postulates*, which are propositions that, in addition to *not* having been demonstrated, do not even seem self-evident. They are, at most, parts of a general rule of logical thought. If this is the case with mathematics, what can we expect from our heritage of family, political, historical and sexual knowledge?

For something to be incorporated into the cognitive heritage of science, it must first be sifted through a rigorous series of tests selected by epistemology and editorial zeal. But, before modern science incorporated into the cognitive heritage its new achievements, discoveries, rules of admission[10] and more relentless statistical tests, that collection was not empty. We know that our heads are full of myths because there was a time in the distant past of our species when those myths were necessary. We have already alluded to the fact that the human mind is prepared to accept almost anything, as long as it is presented as an explanation, and especially if that explanation is given to us by an authority. But why were these myths necessary? The comparative study of a multitude of peoples and the religions and myths they generated indicates that society promoted myths to foster, to encourage, to urge the countryman to be altruistic, to cooperate, to have a reciprocal attitude with the other members of the tribe. The great guarantor of the myths was ultimately God. This imagined God, with all legislative, executive and judicial power in his hands, shamed and accused anyone who violated any social norm and could even have him or her expelled from the tribe or even killed. That is why, in my book on sons of bitches, I point out that the Agrarian Revolution caused the growth of human groups from 40–50 nomadic hunters where "everybody" knew everybody else, including their relatives,[11] and allowed them to increase numerically to villages, towns and cities with millions of inhabitants, where almost all of the others do not know us and we do not know them, the multitude of "others" around us became unknown, and now, if visual contact with any of them lasts longer than a fraction of a second, long enough to see them and not bump into them, it is considered hostile. We no longer know the lying, lazy, bad friend *personally*. Myths diluted their power: the tribal God did not go global. Now, our cognitive heritage is an illusory bag of cats that will have a rigid epistemological control at the current, professional end, where we carefully load it with new knowledge from rigorous scientific research, but that, in the past, was exposed for years to our admitting anything, especially when we were children. On the other hand, no one can take away with reasons concepts that were not incorporated in a reasoned way. In his book *On the Genealogy of Morality*, Friedrich Nietzsche writes: "Perhaps there is nothing more terrible and strange in man's prehistory than his *technique of mnemonics*".[12]

Finally, it is essential to bear in mind that biological organisms, from viruses to human beings, are cheats by nature; we resort to clothes, hairstyles, perfumes, make-up, language, feathers, crests, changes of colour and a thousand other tricks[13] to emphasise differences from or similarities with the "other" and induce them to accept that, in reality, we have a different identity and, except in very favourable circumstances, it will be too risky for them to trust us blindly.

Is It Possible to Keep Our Appetites and Prejudices in Check?

Let us put ourselves for a moment in the mind of a Christian in the Middle Ages. He understood perfectly well that he should not hate his parents, kill, steal, get drunk, lust after his neighbour's wife, masturbate or lie, and he promised on his knees not to sin again. But both he and his confessor knew that his body would make him relapse and, if left unchecked, would surely condemn him to hell. So, in a supreme effort to keep that sinful body in check, he fasted, slept on pebbles, wore hair shirts, walked barefoot on icy stones and did not bathe; it was said that he would "die in the odour of sanctity" when his agonised body reeked horribly. Caterina da Siena gave herself three lashes a day until she bled. For a similar purpose, Louis IX of France (the future Saint Louis) wore hair shirts, which were found embedded in his flesh when he was prepared for burial. They treated their own bodies like their farm animals, which they castrated, harnessed and whipped, so that the animal, instead of doing what its nature urged it to do, would do what the master commanded. And not even their judgement, their ethics, their fear of hell could restrain their cravings.

We should not think for a moment that flesh rules and behaviour obeys. The fact that, in each group of chimpanzees, there is only one dominant male, and the rest of the males are prepubescents who will not dispute anything with the leader is a coincidence that, at the time, raised suspicions and, when the mechanism was unravelled, caused admiration. How can they dispute, if the dominant male is twice the size of a prepubescent, much more robust and has killer fangs! Curiously, if for whatever reason this male disappears – say, because he was hunted and devoured by a feline – within 2 or 3 months a replacement emerges and develops quickly and in a timely manner. It happens that the *fear* of the dominant male meant that the prepubescent brain could not instruct the pituitary gland to secrete gonadotrophins, and their gonads did not mature; now, however, in the absence of the old male, the brain stops inhibiting the neuroendocrine system, gonadotrophins reach the testes, and a big, fanged male is produced in no time at all. An even more obvious example of this multiple interdependence between brain, mind, body, feelings and senses is given by Vilayanur Subramanian Ramachandran's discovery of phantom limb pain. An amputee, who has lost, say, the right forearm, has intolerable pain in the missing forearm (hence the name "phantom limb", as it does not exist but still hurts). Ramachandran devised a box in which the patient places his or her remaining arm and can look down from above. He or she sees the left arm where it is and also sees it on the right side, where the right arm is missing, only it is the mirror image of the left one. In short, he or she sees the image of two arms: the one he or she really has and the one represented by the mirror image. It was discovered that the brain was looking for his or her right arm, because it interprets the signals it receives from the severed nerve endings in the stump as "assuring" it that this right arm exists. But it cannot see it because it is actually missing. The pain arises from a kind of protest by the brain, because of the discrepancy between feeling an arm and not being able to see it. It seems that the lack of sense not only puzzles: it hurts. Instead, doctor and patient now make the brain believe that both arms are there, just as it feels, and this lie is enough to mitigate the pain. This invites us to ponder whether the prejudiced liar is lying *to himself* in the first place, because he feels he is better off.

We are not even in charge of ourselves! To see this in all its hopelessness, let us introduce the doppelgänger. The recording methods used in modern physiology are very fast and subtle. One hundred-metre sprinters have donned a headband with a recorder that transmits wirelessly to a receiver held by a neurobiologist. They are crouched, ready to run as soon as the judge fires the gun. The shot is fired, but they remain crouched and motionless, because, from the time their eardrums began to vibrate from the bang until the acoustic nerve carried the information to the brain, and the brain set in motion some circuits that decode the signal and send nerve impulses to the muscles to start the run, a few milliseconds (between 60 and 120 milliseconds) passed. Only then do the athletes start running, but, here is the funny thing: the runners only realise that they are running at about 300 milliseconds. They only realise it a quarter of a second after the bullet has been fired! Who then gave the order for the athletes' bodies to start running? The answer is the doppelgänger, whom we can imagine as a sort of *other self*, "someone" who dwells in the brain, some set of integrated nuclei perhaps, who decides to set it running and, moreover, being very kind, sends the warning to certain brain centres of the athletes, so that they indulge in the *belief* that it is they, their consciousnesses, who have decided that they should run. Of course, we all have a doppelgänger, just like these runners. Everyone knows that this doppelgänger is also much more skilful and powerful than "us" (than our conscience). To convince us, let us think of a harpist; his consciousness is not quick and skilful enough to say "I will pluck the 14th string with the index finger of the right hand, while the ring finger plays the 16th and the rest of the fingers of that hand are held in the air; in turn, the thumb of the left hand …". Let us convince ourselves, we have neither the speed nor the finger-by-finger control to play the harp; the real performer is the doppelgänger; our consciousness had better not intrude and interfere with it while it is playing a piece. Back to the prejudice: the doppelgänger has shown signs of walking the neural heights, with the ability to cause a gap in the mind of the one about to commit murder, and to cause the criminal to go into fulminant cardior-espiratory arrest before he pulls the trigger – and yet he does not do it. This leads us to ask how many things our doppelgänger will decide and on the basis of what criteria, for which society then holds "us", those of us who speak and write these essays, responsible.

From the Primordial Soup to the Individual and to the Collective Subject

Life began on the planet as a single nutrient soup where trillions of molecules collided, reacted chemically and stuck together in molecular clumps that exchanged products and reagents with neighbouring clumps and split again. Until then, there were no species, no organisms and no individuals. Suddenly, at various points in that succulent sea, tiny droplets began to appear, clois-tered and isolated in compartments lined with biological membranes. Today, we have hard evidence that we are descended from that *single* chemical pro-cess, that, once fragmented, these droplets began to recognise themselves as organisms endowed with life. I call it hard evidence because we still share with rhinoceroses, cockroaches, goldfinches and amoebas *the same* 20 or so species of amino acids, which are assembled into proteins with a *unique* genetic code imprinted in DNA and RNA, drawing on the *very same* molecules of ATP, ADP, phosphates and the whole molecular repertoire of life. The incredible diversification of life would eventually produce millions of different species (bacteria, camels, jasmines, orangutans, ferns) descended from that ancestral soup. Today, this identity of basic chemical components is further proof that it was a *communal* beginning, and life remains unique because, as far as we know, there is only *one* phenomenon on our globe that we can call "life".[14] So, when human beings chose to integrate into societies and began to suffer from a multitude of restrictions, they must have suffered a "cultural *malaise*", but it is obvious that it was a reunion because, long before, we had emerged as a species, *Homo sapiens*, at one point, and from there we were dispersed all over the planet, so that today we depend on this "*well-being* of belonging to a single life".[15] In other words, the growth of human groups (from the small nomadic tribe to the primitive settlements made possible by the Agrarian

Revolution, and from these to the multitudes that today swarm in cities) may have caused us discomfort by restricting our individual freedoms, but we continue to live thanks to the well-being that comes from our having been together to begin with.

Now, as if the complexity of a single individual (a single person) were not enough, we must remember that populations are not simple repetitions of the same essential type, and that the behaviour of a society is far more complex than the simple sum of the behaviour of each of its members when they are isolated. Among other things, the integration of individuals gives rise to so-called *emergent properties*,[16] which are traits that could not have been predicted on the basis of the properties that the individuals had before they were mixed and systematised. An example often given by teachers is the following: chlorine is a poisonous gas, and sodium is a mild, highly reactive metal, and from analysing them separately you would not suspect that when they come together (sodium chloride) they would have the emergent property of making us taste salty. Studying the neurons that appear in the early gestational stages of a human embryo, it is impossible to predict that, as they proliferate, differentiate and integrate into circuits, they will form the brain of a billiard player, a murderer or a bricklayer.

It is common for prejudice to be linked to perversity, and for the degree of human perversity to show great variations throughout prehistory and history, attributable as a rule to great, irreversible changes (i.e. wars, crises, the Agrarian Revolution, the French Revolution, the Industrial Revolution).[17] Just as there are no poor/rich animals and plants, before the Agrarian Revolution, human beings were not divided in this way either. One of the emergent properties of that exaggerated increase in the number of human beings was the emergence of poverty. Later, not only did this asymmetry in the distribution of money distinguish them, but poverty has drastically affected food, education, the causes of disease, and the type and degree of crimes that humans commit, to such an extent that a visitor from another planet would say that an extremely rich human being and an extremely poor human being do not seem to belong to the same biological species. The degree of perversity prevailing at any given time does not merely *cause* this differentiation, it then also causes rich and poor to have a different attitude towards each other, and to attribute the difference to the most capricious variables, such as race, nationality, social class, education, which are interwoven to such a degree that, once mixed together, it becomes practically impossible to distinguish them, a circumstance that becomes a powerful generator of ad hoc prejudices. From then on, people act as if certain prejudices are essential components of the national being and fear that, if the prejudices on which they now rely were to crumble, the fabric of their culture and identity would collapse, and they would turn their backs on the fathers of the nation who may have lived and died to generate those founding prejudices. But, if that is the case, what is the advantage of hoarding mistakes and embedding them in society as prejudices?

Well-being in Culture

The tradition of assuming that an animal does not feel, does not suffer, and can be castrated, whipped and exploited with impunity had highly cultured and depraved champions such as Descartes,[18] and even today some people still assume that the (human) "other" is necessarily a selfish, brutal subject, an execrable enemy, and it is reflected in the expressions we use to refer to this "other", such as "primitive", "rustic", "wild", "barbarian", "fierce", "coarse", "irrational", "uncouth", "rough", "bestial", which make up a repertoire of prejudices. Today, however, biology assigns an indispensable role to the "other", to the point that our life continues to depend on it, as there is no ecological niche composed of a single species: *without the other, there is no life.* This is not without terrible consequences, such as machismo, slavery and filicide.

The existence of "others" is so valuable that life resorts to forging them and then taking advantage of their existence. There are algae cells that can differentiate[19] into different cell types (become "other") only when they proliferate and group together above a certain number, after which each type performs a distinct and indispensable function for the group, and some varieties appear among them that go on to emit light. A human mother can gestate a foetus-baby in 9 months, which is an "other" with whom, during pregnancy and after birth, a very rich exchange of substances and messages takes place. If *the baby* did not suckle, *she* would not secrete milk. It is obvious that, once the baby is born, mother and child send each other highly complex flows of signals that coordinate their neural, endocrine and postural circuits even while both are asleep, and this modulates the development of both. A final example, that of the so-called "wolf children" who, if they manage to survive, are underdeveloped and asocial, reminds us that the quality of being human is also conferred on us by the collective we form with others.[20]

The Superbrain and Its Ways of Interpreting Reality

When *Homo sapiens* gather, they can express emergent properties by adding their minds together so that, between them, they can manufacture what, for lack of a better expression, we will call "group processor" or "group brain" or, more simply, "superbrain", which has with our personal brain the same relationship that our computer has when we access Google, internet, bibliographic services; that is to say, we still have autonomy, but now we benefit from the fact that our terminal has been able to integrate itself into a "machine to learn and even to think", that our brain takes advantage of its integration into a network of computers, servers, monstrously large memories distributed in processors located in several countries at the same time. But then this assembly of people becomes a sort of big brother, father and hierarchical superior who stipulates how we should behave in that flock, how we should combine local foods in our diet to maintain our health, what we should sow, what time of year we should fertilise the soil, when to water, which god we should worship, which *official history* we should adopt and, naturally, which institutions and sets of laws we should obey to remain part of our horde. These networks are a veritable vade mecum of recipes, memories, scientific and civil laws, fashions, handbooks, dossiers that preserve our personal data and the grades we received in high school; among so many good things, they also contain outdated ideas that have proved to be erroneous and even shameful, but we cannot ignore or fail to comply with them as long as successive generations do not change them. In short, we have the power to algebraically add up our discomforts and fortunes in culture, to generate our own hierarchical superior, in which the emergent properties become important.

My brain, your body. The comparison of the immense efficiency that a computer achieves when connected to networks gives us an idea of why human beings, who have made the ability to interpret our tool for survival, tend to associate in groups. But it may lead us to think that this is exclusively a matter of greater versatility, memory capacity, access to a diversity of programs or information immensity. However, there is something human about the group that allows it to escape the strict analogy with a computer: *authoritarianism.* In her studies of evil, Hannah Arendt[21] refers to the survival instinct of a grey, nondescript bureaucrat such as Adolf Eichmann, without much cultural or political interest, who – as he himself confessed – never killed a Jew with his own hands, led him to docilely obey his superiors, swallow his doubts, silence his compassion, put on a blindfold to shut out reality, and carry on unquestioningly loading old men, young men, women and children on to long trains en route to the gas chambers. "The terrible thing about Eichmann", Arendt pointed out, "is that he was not an exceptional man, but an ordinary man, which means that *every ordinary man* can become an Eichmann." I have emphasised the words "every ordinary man" to return to my suspicion that we are then dealing with a biological universality, that of being a potential evil, and the drama was that this *potential* human condition was activated when put in the right circumstance: Nazism. We are, then, faced with a rare property of the brain: the mind of an authoritarian character (i.e. Eichmann's superiors) can invade the brain of a fainthearted person, shut it down and then use his body as a puppet. What makes matters worse is that it seems to be a property of transitive character, because, after all, Eichmann would obey his superiors, but then he had hosts of subordinates who obeyed him. But be warned: once the situation was set up, there was no need for the hierarchs to pass on *their* prejudices to him, for, at this point in the chain of transmission, it was enough that there were orders-that-were-dictated-to-an-obedient-person.

Complex Systems

In the early days of modern science, it was customary to analyse natural phenomena by isolating them from reality, simplifying and "purifying" them until a single cause, *the* cause, stood out, especially when the relationship between this cause and the effect it produces was linear and continuous. But problems arose; for example, an electric current can flow owing to a difference of electric potential (its main cause), but also a difference of *temperature* between two points of the system can make an electric current flow, and, vice versa, a heat flow can flow owing to a difference of temperature between two points, but also owing to a difference of electric potential between those points. In a word, one cause can give rise to many effects, and, conversely, one effect can be due to several causes, which can act in isolation or simultaneously.[22] But the most serious drawback arises when one tries to reintegrate into reality what has been learned with the portions of that reality that have been artificially and experimentally isolated for study. Today, however, the opposite approach prevails: we must first of all find out whether the system we are interested in is a *complex system*, in which so many different components interact that they cannot be studied in a single scientific discipline. Well-known examples of complex systems are death,[23] life, climate, society, public health, science.[24] For example, the famous Strasbourg church clock tells the time, the day of the week, the month, the season of the year, the phase of the moon and so on. But, even so, it is not considered *complex* but *complicated*, because it can be studied using only one discipline: mechanics. If prejudice has biological and non-biological, conscious and unconscious, personal and population, current and many centuries-old components, it is a strong candidate for us to approach it as a complex system. One of the characteristics of complex systems is that they give rise to emergent properties, which we have already discussed.

One of the complex systems that could not have been generated without a huge accumulation of people of different qualities is modern science. Imagine what would happen if humanity were suddenly touched with a magic wand that would make everything due to modern science and advanced technology disappear instantly. In 1 week, more than three-quarters of the population would die – we mean all the diabetics who depend on insulin, the heart patients who depend on hypotensive drugs and pacemakers, patients who wander around with their oxygen tanks, those who would freeze to death if their heating was turned off or starve to death trapped on the top floors of skyscrapers, or simply the entire population of a city whose electrical power comes from generating plants hundreds of kilometres away and whose food is carried frozen from hundreds or thousands of kilometres away. Let us remember that, during the Stone Age, a human being lived only 20–24 years, and today we can live more than 80 years, depending on the technical resources and care that our culture has developed. All this is "known" to the collective, the group processor or superbrain, and it knows that it can only maintain this situation on condition that it is undisturbed and obeyed, that *its* judgements are obeyed and not necessarily those of the individuals who compose it when they are isolated. This tribal brain then empowers us to come up with things that, on our own, we might not dare to do. Many of them are positive and altruistic, but they can also be atrocious, such as convincing us that we should burn down a Jewish quarter, lynch a black man, stone a woman who dared to leave the house with her face uncovered, take a knife and remove the clitoris of little girls so that, when they grow up, they will not sin, or eliminate women who want to have access to education like the men of their village. The harness of demands that have been put on us and that we must endure in order to continue belonging to this "group processor", the tools people use to manipulate us are called "upbringing", "primary school", "university", "temple", "police", "political party". They all have their conditions of admission, all upper levels apply restrictions to the lower levels, and all together impose a price for admitting us to belong.

Religions as Sources of Prejudice

Given that effective interpretation of reality is essential for survival, one of the things that *Homo sapiens* did as soon as consciousness sprouted, only about 50,000–60,000 years ago, was to add it to the effort to interpret reality (which, of course, it was already doing unconsciously), generating successive conscious mental models. Thus, it went from animisms to polytheisms, from there to monotheisms, and – in the case of Christianity – by propitiating its transformation into the religion of the Roman state, Constantine seems to have forced a syncretism with the millenary paganism with which this empire was already managed and ended up degrading it into Roman Catholicism – that is, it returned to a polytheism. Each transition required a gigantic cognitive step, the detail of which we will not go into here. In the course of this evolution from one model of interpreting reality to another, we have arrived at the one that is most effective today – *modern science*, which is the first form that does not evoke deities or miracles to explain why the sky is starry or why the gestation of a child takes 9 months. But it would be impossible for the whole of humanity to synchronise the evolution of its ways of interpreting reality through animistic, polytheistic and monotheistic models, and for everyone to simultaneously accede to the scientific model as if it were possible to declare (and put into practice) "Tonight at zero hour we will pass from polytheisms to monotheisms; or from monotheisms to the scientific way". Moreover, it is not true that a person is an animist *or a* polytheist *or a* monotheist, but that each of us has remnants of all these ways of interpreting reality. In the middle of the 21st century, I hear of a neighbour standing next to the raised bonnet of his car, giving vent to his anger and going so far as to punch it: "This damn engine won't start!" Not only does he attribute his mishap to a wish of the engine's soul, but he curses it and punishes it. For this reason, whatever remains of animism in the population plus whatever remains of polytheism and monotheism are added up at all times. And this does not emerge *as judgement* – that is, reasoned arguments that the car has a soul and a will and that it will be corrected for fear of another beating – but suddenly acts as if there were an explicit prior agreement: a prejudice.

Science does not admit dogmas or the principle of authority. This means that it has no truths either, because all its statements are exposed to the possibility that, in a month or three centuries, someone will discover that we have made a methodological error or a flaw in the chain of reasoning that leads to each conclusion, or that a better way of interpreting it will appear. This peculiarity of scientific knowledge means that science not only advances by incorporating the novelties provided by systematic research and fortuitous discovery, but also spends its time searching for internal inconsistencies within its patrimony of knowledge and eliminating them, as if there were a real immune system in charge of watching over cognitive purity. This is why, in Italian, French and English, research is called *ricerca*, *recherche* and *research*, which emphasise this searching and searching again. On the other hand, ways of interpreting reality that require recourse to deities (i.e. Roman paganism, Christianity, Catholic polytheism, Jewish monotheism) lack a system of self-correction similar to the scientific one. Worse, since the encyclical *Quanta Cura*, promulgated in 1864 by Pope Pius IX, popes are considered infallible, and since then there is no way to correct a dogma that a pope has promulgated. Contrast this with the view of the logician and economist William Stanley Jevons, who argued that, while progress depends on the incorporation of new knowledge and advanced conceptual schemes, it also lies in the elimination of errors, misconceptions and gross authoritarianism.

Science spends its days obsessively self-exploring for inconsistencies, discrepancies between what its various disciplines say, and also demanding the epistemological rules by which it accepts the information that each one brings it with a view to converting it into knowledge. One of its obsessions is with so-called "artefacts" – that is, signals that do not come, for example, from the hormone molecule being studied, but from the solvent or from not having kept the bottle in a refrigerator. These are of no interest to us here. On the other hand, we are interested in bringing up the *placebo again*. Many years ago, in order to find out whether a drug really had the effect it was supposed to have, it was tested on a group of patients; if they felt better, the drug was accepted. This procedure was criticised, and patients were then divided into two groups: one group was given the drug, and the other was not, and the results were then compared. This procedure was also criticised, as the mere act of administering or not administering the drug influenced the patient and conditioned the type of result obtained ("*placebo effect*"). Then the procedure was changed to giving bottles of pills with the drug to a group of doctors and bottles of identical pills without the drug to other doctors, so that these doctors did not know whether the pill they were administering contained the drug. It was the researchers who had distributed the bottles to the doctors who had recorded the relevant information and kept it hidden until the end ("double-blind systems"). But even so, they did not consider the differences between administering or not administering the drug to be valid. The reason is that, in a population, there are suddenly false positives and false negatives that make it possible to obtain or not to obtain the effects by chance. Only the increase in the number of samples was ensuring that mere chance did not play a role. Those who fill in the cognitive gaps with invocations of miracles, revelations and chance occurrences do not take such precautions to exclude placebo effects. In other words, human beings turn to mitigating their anxieties in the face of the unknown by resorting to *cognitive placebos,* and this ensures that the religious artefacts that so blight the quality of life and morale of humanity will spread.

This internal struggle against falsehood establishes a crucial difference from religions, whose strategy has been, on the other hand, to prevent the parishioner from being insubordinate to the authority that forces him to believe in a certain phenomenon, historical fact, character and so on. It is difficult to exaggerate the role of religions in human intellectual progress, as they *were* essential stepping stones in the unstoppable evolution of ways of interpreting reality; that is, they were at the time the best scheme that could be forged with the knowledge that existed – at the time – when each one prevailed. In the case of Western civilisation, it was from Christianity that the Renaissance *and no less than modern science* emerged, music subtly and intellectually developed in its structure, notation, instruments, advanced vocal techniques of singing and modern musical forms, and, finally, without those ways of interpreting that were religious predecessors of science, we would not have modern science today. But the fact that religions lack a mechanism to search and research for inconsistencies, expel errors and guard against placebo effects, plus the elastic and figurative use of metaphors, transformed religious corporations into living fossils, which claim (and get!) the right to educate children with conceptual schemes in abrupt discrepancy with reality. Societies still do not give children the right to have their mental health respected and their brains not raped and abused by adults with cognitive noise. Prejudiced teaching goes as far as violating natural laws as well as national laws. For example, a little boy is brought to his knees and punched in the chest until he admits that he is guilty of a mythical couple (Adam and Eve) having eaten an apple, when today the laws of the country do not allow a person to be convicted for misdeeds committed by a great-great-grandfather. Then, this teaching based on falsehoods convinces him that he is a sheep in the Lord's flock, even though, at that very moment, his country's teachers are trying to turn him into a *citizen* who thinks and expresses himself on the basis of his knowledge and his rights. Not even the most foolish utopian has ever imagined a democracy for sheep. Moreover, in strident contradiction to the development of ethics pursued by a modern society, religious teaching threatens these citizens with brutal and eternal torture in hell, whereas one of the greatest problems of a modern state is to educate the child so that when she or he becomes an adult citizen, she or he will not allow their society or their government to torture prisoners – or anybody, in fact. Even those citizens have their dignity destroyed and are subjected to a brutal ethical conflict when they are forced to *love* a deity who went so far as to demand the sacrifice of his own son (Christ) on condition of forgiving a supposed offence to his authority. So, these cognitively erroneous and morally monstrous antiquities are reservoirs of prejudice and corruption that cause many of the greatest calamities afflicting humanity, fauna, flora and the entire planet.

The Importance of Being (Prejudiced) Believers in Culture and History

The sense of time allows us to make dynamic models of reality, and these help us adapt to both the present and the future and even learn what happened 13.7 billion years in the past! That is why *Homo sapiens* were selected with longer and longer temporal arrows. Eventually, the length of the time arrow generated by *Homo sapiens made* her realise that there would be a time when she would perish. Just as she felt security and confidence when she could interpret reality and know how it would be convenient for her to handle herself in the future, the ignorance of what her fate would be after she died tormented her. But it was here that the capacity to be believers came to the fore, when the culture to which she belonged led her to believe that the universe is governed by deities who would shower her with happiness if in life she had behaved in a certain way (paradises), obeyed certain laws and performed the rites indicated by their priests, or else she would be condemned to merciless punishments (hells) if her life had gone astray, if she had not observed the rules instilled by her elders, her society, her authorities.

When we are born, that religion is already there, in the hands of priests and powerful people who "explain it to us" and attest that paradise and hell await us. As we can see, we owe our lives, our sanity and even our civilisation to our ability to be (prejudiced) believers.

The Social Superbrain Is Very Jealous of Its Purity

I recognise that, in likening the superbrain to a computer, I am exaggeratedly demeaning it, because computers only manage algorithms devoid of emotions, sexual and food cravings, love, self-sacrifice, aesthetic inclinations and the rest of the human qualities that, on the contrary, are variables that a human being can manage. But I do so because this "human computer" is a colossal storehouse of data and computational capacity that resembles an extra-personal intelligence that is very actively involved in human affairs. Nor does it take much to realise that we may belong to as many different superbrains or group brains as there are combinations of people we can integrate, for I am sure there are superbrains to which I belong (those of doctors, molecular and cellular physiologists, Spanish-speakers, music lovers, chess players, people born in Argentina) and superbrains that would not incorporate me because I do not belong (military, priests, violinists, Czechs, mountaineers, morticians, bullfighting lovers). And here I stop fantasising, because all I wanted to say is that these superbrains to which we belong do not allow themselves to be approached and integrated by anyone just like that. To prove it, observe how institutions, businesses, banks, ministries, countries do it, programming their computers to protect their integrity, demanding our name and surname, passport, visas, photos, fingerprints, postal address and passwords, to admit us as users.

Guarding the purity of our organism is so important that we tend to isolate, encapsulate and eliminate any object (thorn, suture thread, pellet, parasite) that is embedded in our organism, but that the organism does not recognise as its own. This control and strategy seem to continue in social groups; even human computers are extremely jealous of not being contaminated by characters who try to intrude. It must be crucial that it then generates "proof of belonging" through which it can satisfy its status – are you one of us or not? A very different fate awaits us depending on whether we answer "yes" or "no". It seems as if peoples have traditionally equipped themselves with walls of prejudice, and that our proving to them that we, as individuals, have incorporated, value and obey those same prejudices is far more valuable than a simple magnetic ID card.

Perhaps, among the uses of prejudice to which I have referred in previous pages, I should have included a brief description from Sternberg and Sternberg's book, *The Nature of Hate*,[25] referring to the fact that, at the time, Germans, Soviets and Americans generated prejudices and used them to mount propaganda campaigns to insert into the minds of *their own citizens*, which made it easier for the states to enlist them in wars that, had it not been for those packs of lies, might have been avoided.

Thomas Malthus and the Most Powerful and Sublime Placebo of Them All

Thomas Malthus has proposed (and two and a half centuries of biological science have demonstrated) that species can produce far more progeny than the available living space and food can keep alive. This forces each species to fight among its own and make sure that the "other" will perish or at least not be able to procreate more than "one". This was already done by mindless ancestral species. By the time we *Homo sapiens* emerged as a biological species with refined mental capacities, we were already programmed to be potential *genocidaires*. Prejudice is one of the many manifestations of this war of "one against the other", from which we will not be able to desert because, by the way, we are also born with this susceptibility to be injected with these huge doses of prejudice that generations and generations before us have prepared for us. The prefix pre-in *prejudice* does not allude to us, it does not include us, it only indicates that the family, the country, society has engraved it on us during child-hood – that is, when we were passive subjects, and the concepts were engraved on us because nature has endowed us with a recordable mind. Then, as one of their many properties, prejudices redouble their poison because, rather than opposing reasons, they can infiltrate them – both those of others and our own – until they achieve a goal: to serve as a platform for whoever has the authority and strength to impose them.

I believe that the prejudiced person cannot be cured; at most they learn to hypocritically hide their prejudices, to join in demonstrations in which they shout loudly "*Never again!*", knowing that they are merely making faces, which never go beyond the headlines. Nevertheless, it is possible to prevent prejudice: Malthus issued his biological sentence with complete clarity, religions have left us the most devastating, powerful and sublime placebo ever imagined: God. But science, which is becoming the most powerful resource for *understanding* situations and *solving* problems that we have ever forged, has the capacity to educate in a culture compatible with it, in which the old god-hoax does not appear. For the best, while we speak of "fighting", science does not attack the other, it does not hurt him or her, it does not violate his or her body or dignity. The "fight" does not consist in forbidding someone to hold that $2 + 2 = 19$. It simply instructs the other as early as possible, teaches him or her mathematics so that he or she knows that $2 + 2 = 4$, and the one who said "19" disappears per se. It would seem that all that is needed is for our university students and civil servants to have their spines a little straighter and, instead of generating a culture of information, to generate a culture of knowledge, and for the various specialists who train in philosophy, education, children's law, women's law and economics to have at least a little social solidarity.

In Conclusion

I have brought up the biological aspects of prejudice because, although I suspect them to be as important, if not more so, than the non-biological ones, I do not see that they are given due consideration. But this chapter runs the risk of being taken as a proposition (my proposition to top it all!) that ethics plays *no* role; I do not say so, and I hope the reader will not conclude that it does. Finally, I have hoped that prejudice will be approa-ched scientifically, modern science being the most advanced and effective way of interpreting reality and devising solutions. However, it is worth noting that modern science is far from having provided solutions to all the problems it has addressed. Among them, the mind is proving to be a tough nut to crack. So even exaggerations must be used with restraint.

Notes

1 Sternberg and Sternberg, 2008.
2 Michael Shermer, 2011.
3 Bleger referred to these phenomena as "the myth of immaculate perception".
4 José M. Musacchio, 2012.
5 Musacchio uses the word *imprinting*.
6 Pathologies and monstrosities suddenly become magnifying glasses, microscopes and telescopes that amplify real phenomena and processes and help to discover them. When I was a child, I lived a few metres away from an inn where my childish mind marvelled at discussions like the following: "I'm telling you no!", "And I'm telling you yes!", "But you're a brute: I'm telling you no and you don't understand me!" Child and all, I was astonished that they could argue without arguing, as if they were scientific illiterates from the developing world. In reality, they were.
7 Unfortunately, today's newspapers rely on statistics, not reasoning, on the opinions of film or sports stars, and thus continue to believe that voting is a democratic procedure.
8 This attitude contrasts sharply with that of scientists who seem to live in the expectation that someone will doubt, taking it as a reason to go out and look for more and better evidence.
9 Paul Kurtz, 1997. "It is usually considered to be in bad taste to question the claims of religion."
10 It is said that John Foster Dulles, US Secretary of State, was a hard man to convince. Once, when he was on a train with a group of colleagues, someone pointed to a flock and said: "Look at those freshly shorn sheep". Dulles looked at them and reluctantly conceded: "Well ... from this side."
11 Homer's *Iliad* offers eloquently clear examples that, in the battles between Trojans and Achaeans, each side knew not only their own hosts, but also their fathers and each of their enemies and even their respective fathers. Fragments abound, such as "looking at the warriors, Priam asked me: 'And who is that man?' [...] 'It is Ulysses, I replied, son of Laertes, grown up in Ithaca' [...] 'It is true', said Priam, I met him one day when he came here with Menelaus ... I took him into my house (!)' [...] Then Priam distinguished Ayante ... and said to him 'Arise, son of Laomedonte' [...] Then Menelaus, son of Asclepius [...] Ayante of Telemon hit the young son of Antemion, Simoesius [...] Píroo faced Diores, son of Amarinceo. [...] Idomeneus killed Festus, son of Boron [...] Menelaus, son of Atren, speared Scamandrius, son of Strophios [...] Megeteus killed Pedaeus, who was the bastard son of Antenor". It sounds like a neighbourhood brawl.
12 Friedrich Nietzsche, 1994, p. 38.
13 Loyal Rue, 1994.
14 It is possible that, at times (especially early times), there could have been two or more types of life, but, if that is the case, organisms similar to us have eaten all the others.
15 It should be noted that thanks to this identity due to a common origin, the vast majority of knowledge about how *our* brain, heart and pancreas work comes from studies carried out on an "other" made up of experimental animals. Today, a medical-pharmaceutical industry is not allowed to give us any medicine if it has not been proven that it does not harm "them". For years, we have treated our diabetics with insulin obtained from "their" pancreas, we have fought infections in our bodies with vaccines that were developed in them for us, and we have sutured our wounds with cats' guts.
16 An emergent property is one that appears above a certain level of complexity of a system, and that we could hardly have predicted by extrapolating previous properties. Today, we do not know how cardiocytes (individual muscle cells) come together to generate a whole heart that will coordinate itself to beat and pump

blood with a certain periodicity, or how neurons manage to associate and build the most complex object in the whole universe: the brain.

17 Marcelino Cereijido, 2011.

18 "When he vivisected and inserted tubes into the oesophagus and trachea, or stimulated dissected nerves of dogs tied to the table, he dismissed the convulsions and howls of pain by likening them to a carillon that vibrates and emits sounds without suffering, since neither the carillon nor the dog has a soul."

19 "Differentiation" is the process by which a cell reads and executes the messages of different genes and goes on to adopt different structures and ways of functioning. To get an idea of the importance of differentiation to life, recall that the fertilised egg that gave rise to us not only multiplied millions of times but also produced lineages of cells that gradually differentiated into muscle cells, neurons, adipocytes, lymphocytes, thymocytes and so on.

20 The monk Crescimbene di Parma reports that Frederick II, emperor of the Holy Roman Empire, took newborn babies and entrusted them to a group of wet nurses who were strictly ordered to breastfeed and care for them without speaking a word to the babies or to each other, on pain of death and under the watchful eye of soldiers. The emperor wanted to know what language children who had never heard any human language would start speaking, and so he hoped to find out what language Adam and Eve had spoken. The children died within a very short time, and today, when compared with infants who come to suffer from "hospitalism", it follows that their immune systems (among other systems) must not have matured, and they were killed by infections caused by opportunistic organisms. A child truly isolated from society (not one abandoned at the age of 2 or 3) is unviable, for he or she is not only not humanised but also fails to survive.

21 Hannah Arendt, 1963.

22 In recognition of these developments, Lars Onsager was awarded the Nobel Prize in Chemistry in 1968.

23 Fanny Blanck-Cereijido and Marcelino Cereijido, 2002a, 2002b.

24 Cereijido, 1994, 2009.

25 Sternberg and Sternberg, 2008.

References

Arendt, Hannah, *Eichmann in Jerusalem*. New York, Penguin, 1963.

Blanck-Cereijido, Fanny and Cereijido, Marcelino, *La vida, el tiempo y la muerte* (Life, time and death). Mexico, FCE, 2002.

Blanck-Cereijido, Fanny and Cereijido, Marcelino, *La muerte y sus ventajas* (Death and its benefits). Mexico, FCE, 2002.

Cereijido, Marcelino, *Ciencia sin seso locura doble* (Science without brains double madness) Mexico, Siglo XXI, 1994.

Cereijido, Marcelino, *La ciencia como calamidad* (Science as a calamity). Barcelona, Gedisa, 2009.

Cereijido, Marcelino, *Hacia una teoría general sobre los hijos de puta* (Towards a general theory on sons of bitches). Mexico, Tusquets, 2011.

Kurtz, Paul, "Two sources of unreason in democratic society: the paranormal and religion", in Paul R. Gross, Norman Levitt and M.W. Lewis (Eds.), *The Flight from Science and Reason*. Baltimore, MD, John Hopkins University Press, 1997.

Musacchio, José M., *Contradictions: Neuroscience and Religion*. Berlin, Springer-Verlag, 2012.

Nietzsche, Friedrich, *On the Genealogy of Morality*. New York, Cambridge University Press, 1994.

Rue, Loyal, *By the Grace of Guile*. Oxford, Oxford University Press, 1994.

Shermer, Michael, *The Believing Brain*. New York, Times Books, 2011.

Sternberg, Robert J. and Sternberg, Karin, *The Nature of Hate*. Cambridge, Cambridge University Press, 2008.

Index

* 9 7 8 1 0 3 2 2 7 2 5 3 5 *